WALKING
THE BEAT TO
NIRVANA

WALKING THE BEAT TO NIRVANA

—

By Mervyn Edwards

Foreword by Phil Gormley – Former Chief Constable
of Police Scotland and Norfolk Police

Written by Mervyn Edwards.

First published in the United Kingdom in 2018
by Windlass Publishing Limited (Oxford).

A catalogue record for this book is available
from the British Library.

ISBN – 978-0-9570151-7-3

Printed in the United Kingdom

Windlass Publishing Limited (Oxford)
12 Broad Field Road, Yarnton, Oxford,
OX5 1UL, United Kingdom.

DEDICATION

—

I dedicate this book to my wife Geraldine and my sons Gareth and Matthew.
Without my wife's love, help and total support, especially in the early days
of my career, I could never have achieved any success.

I thank my two sons for their forbearance particularly when they were growing
up and I was missing on so many occasions owing to the nature of 'the job'.

AUTHOR'S NOTE

—

While all events described in the book actually took place, some details, including names and locations, have been changed.

I have been an avid collector of historical cigarette cards for many years. My varied collection covers a number of subjects including, of course, police officers. Each of the chapter headings in this book has one of the images from a W. and F. Faulkner compilation which were first produced in 1899. I hope you agree that they are a fascinating insight into a bygone age.

CONTENTS

—

FOREWORD

—

It was my privilege to serve in Thames Valley Police for the second half of Merv's service, he was a hugely capable and influential senior officer who helped shape the attitudes and careers of many of us lucky enough to have worked with him. Merv was and is a larger than life character who embodied all that is best about British Policing, his professionalism good humour and humanity coupled with a sense of mischief made going to work fun! I know that we were always relieved when Merv and the Support Group turned up, the job would get done and everything would be sorted.

I had heard about Merv long before I met him. I was a young probationary Constable at the time of the 1986 Grendon Underwood prison siege which became the talk of every canteen across the Force. Later as a junior public order commander I saw exactly how good Merv was in a crisis, he had the uncommon attribute of common sense and was always calm and positive no matter how desperate things were.

This book is a fascinating insight into a policing career that bridged decades which saw policing transform in terms of how it had to organise and respond to the mutating threat from armed criminality, terrorism and public disorder. Merv Edwards made a big contribution to this across the three counties of Thames Valley Police, not bad for a Banbury Bus driver!

Phil Gormley QPM

Formerly
Chief Constable Police Scotland,
Deputy Director General NCA,
Chief Constable Norfolk.

ACKNOWLEDGEMENTS

—

I give thanks to the numerous colleagues and friends that I have had the pleasure to work with and alongside for more than 30 years. Thanks go particularly to the many Support Group colleagues, crewmates, supervisors and my teams, those still serving or retired and especially remembering those who are no longer with us. A special mention goes to Glyn Lambert who was a guiding light to me and so many others, he remains a legend in Support Group circles.

In writing this book I thank so many colleagues for their recollections and anecdotes which stir the memories. I will be eternally grateful to Dan and Sarah Clacher for their expertise, help, advice and reassurance without which this book would not have made it this far.

A final special mention to my wife Geraldine whose initial idea it was to write the book. Without her encouragement, suggestions, inspiration and constant re-reads it would never have been written.

LIST OF PHOTOGRAPHS

—

The above listed photographs are reproduced by kind permission of the following; Thames Valley Police 7, 8, 10, 15, 16, Reading Evening Post part of Trinity Mirror Group 4, 19, Bucks Examiner part of Trinity Mirror Group 6, Bucks Advertiser part of Trinity Mirror Group 13, Bucks Free Press 20, Royal Borough Observer part of Newsquest Berks and Bucks 14, Author's photographs 1 Back Cover, 3 Front Cover, 2, 5, 9, 11, 12, 17, 18.

CHAPTER 1

—

1971 Time for a Change

Point duty

I t all started in October 1971 when I had a life changing experience. I joined the Force and became a Police Officer. I was twenty-four years of age and had been married for twelve whole months. I spent all that time living in Banbury and my wife Geraldine and I had just bought a new house in the town. After much discussion between the two of us, I applied to join Thames Valley Constabulary later re-named Thames Valley Police. In fact, I did most of the deliberating and my wife eventually told me to either apply or stop going on about it.

Prior to this, since leaving school aged fifteen, I'd had numerous jobs. I began as a young 'Mr Whippy' working on ice cream vans. Following that I worked for Banbury's leading furnishing company, Chapmans; firstly, as a van boy and then as an apprentice carpet fitter. Once I was considered competent to work on my own, I left Chapmans and was taken on by a local shop to fit carpets in the Oxford area. I was soon bored with this, which led to a period of drifting from job to job. One such niche was delivering bread from door to door, again my round was in Oxford. For a while I was out of work and I bummed around a bit in my flash motor, an Austin A35 van. It was quite notorious around the town due to the authentic blood streak down the length of the driver's door, the result of a disagreement at a local pub. I should have washed it off, but I thought it added a certain kudos, so it stayed on for weeks. It was during this time, whilst hanging around with my best mate Ron and a number of girls from nearby Brackley, that I started going out with my wife to be, Geraldine. That put me back on the path of smartening myself up and getting a 'proper' job again. I found myself in uniform as a bus conductor with the Midland Red bus company and by the age of twenty-one, I qualified as a bus driver, a brilliant job, I loved it.

Happy as I was driving buses, as a schoolboy I'd always wanted to be a policeman and eventually I took the first big step by applying to join the local force.

It was 1971 and I waited nervously for the result of my application to become a police officer. When I received the letter of acceptance, it was a wonderful feeling, yet the short time before I started training was strange. There was the natural apprehension and difficulty in trying to imagine what life as a police officer would be like and a thousand thoughts about how I would deal with different things; traffic accidents, injured people, dead bodies, fights, violence, missing children, anyone hurting children, the list was endless. There was one saving grace however, even before I started my training I thought I had a really good idea of what awaited me and how to deal with certain things. The reason being, Geraldine and I avidly watched Z Cars on TV! It was a very popular programme at the time, but for me it was like a training course and I watched intently to see what to do. I did notice however, that they solved everything within half an hour! Later on, the same principle applied whilst watching John Thaw as Jack Reagan in The Sweeney.

If Z Cars was initial training, The Sweeney was the advanced course. Brilliant.

The training process started with two weeks at Aylesbury Police Station, which included an introduction to the chosen life and issue of uniform and equipment. This was followed by a thirteen-week course at Eynsham Hall near Witney in Oxfordshire. Although it was in Oxfordshire, this was a regional training centre so recruits from many other forces in the UK were sent here too. It was a bit of a culture shock for all of us, in fact it was hell. Before leaving home I, together with the other new recruits, made an effort and we all had, in varying degrees, severe haircuts. Only two of us reported for duty sporting a beard. In 1971 this was fairly new for the Police Force, only twelve months before regulations had changed to allow police officers to wear beards. Phew!!

On arrival at the Police Training Centre we were met by the Drill 'Pig', the all-powerful Drill Sergeant, a frustrated army Regimental Sergeant Major. He informed us that our hair was too long; subsequently we had an appointment every Tuesday evening with the barber who was brought to the centre from his regular place of work at Oxford Prison. There was no excuse for missing the weekly haircut. The said Drill Sergeant, also pointed out that as beards were now allowed in the Police Force he could not make us shave them off (what a relief, great). However, if we both still had beards by 0800 the next morning, we shouldn't bother unpacking. He pointed out where the driveway was which led back to the real world. So that was it, the beard had to go, what trauma! I had worn a beard since I was seventeen years old and my wife of twelve months had never seen me without one.

For the next thirteen weeks the pattern was set: lessons, learning the law, drill, fitness training, first aid, drill, learning how to direct traffic, some sport, more drill, discipline and learning so that you could recite definitions in your sleep. The definitions were especially strange. Everyone was issued with a little yellow book of definitions. These explained what all the terms of criminal law meant. It was important to know what the ingredients were to constitute a theft, what was the difference between a burglary and a robbery and what being a police constable meant. The normal state of affairs was that at break times, lunchtime and evening time, in fact at any time of the day or night you would see hordes of us walking round the grounds with our little yellow books trying to learn the hundred or more definitions...and all this whilst being clean shaven and with almost no hair.

The only relief from these thirteen weeks of hell was on a Wednesday after lessons, we were allowed out on a free evening. Those of us lucky enough to live close by, could go home for a few hours. We had to be back at the centre by 11pm, no staying out all night for any reason. On my first Wednesday evening I travelled home to Banbury, about fifteen miles away. I had warned my wife that I was clean shaven and almost bald headed as well, but when I pulled up on the drive she came to greet me. She took one look at me and immediately closed the door! It was a bit of a shock for us all.

One of the highlights of my time at Eynsham Hall and they were pretty scarce, was being asked to take part in the Christmas Concert. I had become friendly with another new recruit from Banbury, Ron Glynn, and he was very musical. He had previously conducted a band and so 'volunteered' to organise a choir for the concert. I can't imagine how I came to be in such a position, but I found myself taking part. Come the evening of the concert, I was a soloist singing Good King Wenceslas as a tenor. I was part of the 1971 Eynsham Hall Police Male Voice Choir. Claim to fame or what?

The thirteen weeks went very slowly, but we all got through it and soon departed to our various police forces. We had been allocated our postings about half way through the course. I had asked to be posted to Banbury as I was very familiar with the area and I knew the local people, the good and bad. In addition, I had only been married twelve months and Geraldine and I had just bought our own house, a brand new three bedroom property for £3,995; a very strong case for being posted to my home town, one might assume. When I opened the envelope and discovered I had been posted to Chesham, Buckinghamshire, about fifty miles away from Banbury and a place I had never heard of, I wasn't exactly thrilled. Oh joy. I received the posting notice on a Wednesday, just before going home for the evening. I broke the news to Geraldine and we looked Chesham up in the AA book, the Google maps of the day. To our horror Chesham didn't even appear on the map. We later found out that if a town did not have an AA recommended hotel, it didn't appear in the book and that year Chesham didn't have one. What sort of place was this that we were being sent to? We eventually found it was near a town called Amersham. This was where we were going to live.

After my time at Eynsham Hall, I had two weeks Local Procedure Course at Thames Valley Police (TVP) Training Centre at Sulhamstead, near Reading. Having already learnt the laws which apply throughout England and Wales, this concentrated on issues and bye-laws relevant to TVP. For those two weeks there was no contact with the public and more importantly the dreaded drill sergeant, so the harsh beard growth rules were relaxed. Bizarrely whilst beards were technically allowed, they could not be grown whilst on duty if there was any likelihood of contact with the public. Thankfully, my beard slowly re-emerged to a state deemed presentable enough to pass the stringent 'meeting the public test'.

In 1968, the five constabularies of Buckinghamshire, Berkshire, Oxfordshire, Oxford City and Reading Borough had amalgamated to form Thames Valley Constabulary later re-named Thames Valley Police. The diverse nature of the new force contrasting urban conurbations such as Oxford, the new city of Milton Keynes, Reading and Slough with more rural areas, provided many and varied career opportunities. It was thought at the time that this was the blueprint for the future in the UK; many other county forces were expected to amalgamate in this way, but with the notable exception of Scotland it hasn't happened.

We found house prices in Chesham quite a lot higher than in Banbury, so we couldn't afford to buy straight away, my salary being halved by joining the police. We were therefore allocated a police house in Windsor Road, Chesham. We knew the wonderful town of Windsor was not far away. Making our first trip to Chesham and nearing our new address, we were speculating that it was probably on the road to Windsor so maybe would be good. Ha! How wrong can you be? Ours was one of four police houses right in the middle of a large council estate and of course, everyone knew that this was where the coppers lived. Moreover, the estate had a bad reputation - no problem for us, we thought as we were both brought up in council houses.

The house itself was a major issue. We were moving from our brand new modern house to this older place which we soon discovered had stood empty for six months. It needed decorating, the grass in the front garden was about three feet high and as it was January, it was dull and freezing cold. We seriously considered turning it all in there and then, going back to Banbury and seeing if I could get my job back as a bus driver. It was heart-breaking. We were aware of the risk of me joining the police force. We were 22 and 24 years of age, living in Banbury in our own house, newly married and both in jobs we liked. We had decided to throw it all away and move fifty miles to a different county, away from our families, to a place we had never heard of. I was starting in my chosen career in which the pay especially had fallen behind other occupations and conditions needed modernising. In addition my wife was looking for a new job in a place where she knew no-one. The monumental decision of us embarking on this adventure was not taken lightly.

However, we are made of stronger stuff and fortunately we stuck it out because after moving in we found that the police force was selling off lots of police houses and we were able to buy ours at an affordable price.

CHAPTER 2

–

On the Beat

On the beat

My first few weeks and months as a police officer were brilliant, I loved it. I was used to wearing a different uniform as a bus driver. I had a sense of achievement passing my Public Service Vehicle (PSV) test after driver training in a double-decker bus around Birmingham city centre but putting on my police uniform for the first time filled me with immense pride. I was aware that 'The Job' out on the streets really began from here on in. Together with the majority of the population, I always looked with interest whenever I saw a police officer or police vehicle. The public expect the police to deal with difficult incidents and problems, now that police officer would be me! That took some getting used to.

In those days probationers were obliged to walk the beat for about twelve months before they got a driving course. The first three days were spent on patrol with an experienced colleague and then it was out to face the great British public alone. During those three days all the important tea stops were pointed out where police were welcome for a natter and cup of tea. The unusual nature of some properties and the back alleys were also introduced. On night duty I was expected to check all the shops and premises on my beat, physically trying all the doors, front and back. About three months into this I found my first unlocked door, an estate agents in Chesham High Street. After trying door handles for three months and finding them locked, to my surprise this door opened, and I fell in. There was nothing untoward; the owner had just forgotten to lock the front door.

I really enjoyed my time walking the beat. Today's Bobbies don't get that experience and miss out on learning all about their patch. It was an interesting and worthwhile practice. I got to know the local regular cats; one particular black cat near the cinema kept me company on many night shifts. It was a fascinating experience to stand in the middle of the town at 3.00am and hear nothing, not a sound. The quiet was so 'loud' that a leaf could be heard falling through the trees.

Every police officer must serve the first two years of service as a probationary constable before applying for a specialist department. Initially, I quite liked the idea of being a detective on the Criminal Investigation Department (C.I.D.) or perhaps a traffic officer driving fast and powerful cars. I certainly had those recommendations from my sergeants during my probationary period. The idea of being an avuncular village Bobby, riding my bike and having runner beans left on my doorstep appealed too.

All that changed when we had a tragic case of a girl having been murdered at Amersham and the offender was being sought. A Murder Incident Room was set up and a unit of police officers called the Support Group was brought into the area to assist. I had not come across this highly specialised group before. Talking to some of them about their role, I became very interested in their work. They performed a specialised fingertip search at murder and serious crime scenes, conducted house to house enquiries and worked with the Drug Squad and Crime Squads. Their primary function however, was as the Tactical Firearms Team involving them in all firearms incidents. Their place of duty was the whole of the TVP area and they were sent wherever they were needed. I was struck by how fantastic a job it sounded. So enamoured was I by the idea that my mind was made up, that was where I wanted to go next in my career.

I was very fortunate in that my shift at Chesham had a new sergeant appointed who arrived on promotion from that very same Support Group. I was able to hear first-hand all about the department and what I needed to do to join.

I needed experience in a wide range of policing duties. I had spent only a relatively short time at Chesham, my first station, but now had the opportunity to be involved in many varied, interesting, unusual and sometimes tragic incidents.

I was on early turn one morning in 1974 patrolling the Chesham area in a panda car, when just after 9.00am I was directed to Latimer Village near Chesham, after reports of an explosion. It was the site of the National Defence College where senior officers from the three military services received specialist training. On arrival as first police officer on the scene, I could see that there had been an explosion and people had been injured. It soon became apparent that a bomb had been placed against a building and ten people had suffered injuries. The Irish Republican Army (IRA) later claimed responsibility.

There was little training for police in the early '70s for those attending the scene of a bomb blast. There was chaos, confusion and injured people; some serious and others in a state of shock. There were countless things for me to consider, my mind was racing. The injured people, were they safe? What if more of the building collapsed? Was there room for the many ambulances to safely collect the injured and get them to hospital? Would there be space for the fire brigade? Invaluable as they were they had a reputation for parking their fire tenders all over the place. More police assistance was needed and lots of it, scenes of crime staff, CID officers, senior investigators and many more uniformed police. There were numerous roles to fulfil and a desperate need to set up a cordon. Most important, was to preserve what was now a major crime scene and ensure that all the people who were milling about didn't inadvertently walk away with important evidence on their clothes and shoes. One question remained. With so many people in a vulnerable position, were those responsible for placing the bomb still in the vicinity? This was my first experience of a terrorist incident but regrettably, not my last.

One of the major commitments for TVP was the protection of VIPs including the Royal Family and The Prime Minister and other government ministers. In fact, anyone who needed protection and deemed to be at risk.

One such person subject to protection was Lord Peter Carrington, then Defence Secretary and later Foreign Secretary, who lived at Bledlow Ridge. Sometimes, we were required to supplement the protection officers and I performed duty there several times. I enjoyed these tasks at his country house. The grounds were beautiful, and Lord Carrington and his family were especially friendly and very understanding of having a uniformed police officer patrolling their grounds. His youngest daughter, Virginia was particularly friendly. Early on summer mornings, she would call 'good morning' from her window and ensure that I had been served coffee.

An example of how good the Italian staff were, was when I was having a break in their rest room and watching a cookery programme on TV. The housekeeper and cook were working and watching too; the TV chef was making zabaglione. I had never heard of it. I must have said how good it looked because twenty minutes later a bowl of zabaglione was put in front of me to try. It was fabulous, and it was all for me!

One time I arrived for a late turn duty, 2.00pm until 10.00pm, only to be met by Lord Carrington telling me that there had been an accident involving his personal protection officer. Apparently, they had been working on some trees and collecting branches in the nearby woods and the officer had fallen from a tree, injured his shoulder and been taken to hospital. Lord Carrington assured me that the Metropolitan Police at Scotland Yard had been informed. They were trying to identify a replacement to come out to Bledlow Manor, but he had convinced them one was not required. In his words, "I am sure we can manage, can't we?"

"Well if you say so, and if the Met are sure, then I suppose it will be okay," I responded. That settled that then.

His parting shot to me was, "Oh by the way, the Prime Minister, (who was Edward Heath at that time), will be calling round later this evening, just so you are aware."

Sure enough, around 7.00pm the Prime Minister arrived. Soon he and the Defence Secretary were inside enjoying themselves, whilst I walked the grounds responsible for their security. I remember thinking that if this shift goes well, fine, but if not it could be severely career limiting. Thankfully, the evening passed without incident.

In 1974 there was a General Election and Labour gained power. The new Prime Minister was Harold Wilson and Chequers, the PM's country home, and his own house, Home Farm, were very close to Chesham. Sometimes, we were required to do duty at one or other of these locations. My first duty at the PM's home was on a week-end and it was his birthday. The police post was a caravan in the grounds very close to the road and I had been on duty for about an hour when one of the PM's staff informed me that the Prime Minister would like to see me in his study. WHAT! This was the Prime Minister wanting to see me. What could I possibly have done wrong in the short time I had been there? Was the Tower of London still in use for upsetting the Prime Minister? With much trepidation, I went to Harold Wilson's study, knocked the door and he invited me in. This was me in the PM's study chatting with the Prime Minister. He asked me to inform the small gathering of press photographers waiting outside in the road for a birthday photograph of the PM that he would not be appearing during the day, so to avoid wasting their time they could leave if they wished. And that was it, WOW! I could take to this protection lark. Pumped up with my own importance, I promptly delivered the message.

I was a little disappointed the next day when scanning the national papers not to discover any reference to, 'reporting from the Prime Minister's home a police spokesman said', etc…

I went on to perform duties at the PM's home a number of times. I rarely had other dealings with Harold Wilson but did have more with his wife Mrs Mary Wilson, who was a lovely lady. Most encounters with a family member were with Paddy, the golden Labrador. He tended to be overweight, maybe because he knew that those people in blue uniforms spending most of their time walking round the grounds sometimes went back to their caravan and ate sandwiches there. It was hard to ignore those pleading eyes. He was a great favourite and we were only too pleased to help look for him when he went walkabout.

The duties of police officers cover a whole spectrum of situations: comical, boring, difficult, frustrating, tragic, gruesome, heart-breaking, frightening and satisfying. During my time at Chesham I experienced most of those and in one shift from 1400 – 2200 hours, I had more than my fair share for one day's patrol.

I was on mobile patrol alone when shortly after starting duty, I was directed to an area of railway line between Amersham and Great Missenden. There had been a spate of copper wire thefts alongside the railway line. British Transport Police, who had responsibility for policing railways, placed alarms at various points on a long part of the rail system. They were unable to attend immediately, as they were travelling from Baker Street in London. They could not tell us exactly where the alarm had been triggered, but it had been activated somewhere on that stretch of line.

I parked up in the woods about halfway between Amersham and Great Missenden and finding no obvious signs of activity, I climbed down the embankment and started walking alongside the line towards Great Missenden. I had asked for someone else to cover further back towards Amersham. By now it was raining, and I had checked for about two miles to a point where I could see the station. There was no sign of any offenders or any obvious copper wire tampering, so I crossed the track and checked the other side on my way back to the car. The radio reception was sporadic in that area and by the time I got back to the police car it was getting dark, pouring with rain and I had no positive result to report on the copper wire.

It was about 5.00pm, I was due for a break and looking forward to getting into the warm and drying off. As I got into the car and tried to check in on the radio, I received a broken message which sounded something like a reported, 'plane crash.' It couldn't possibly be.

I drove on towards Chesham for a better radio reception where I could hear the message more clearly; I was asked to attend a plane crash. A small plane had come down in woods close to St Leonards village, near Chesham on the very rural Hertfordshire border near Tring. I made my way there and found the fire brigade in attendance, and it was as reported, 'plane crashed in woods in the foul weather, all occupants dead.'

Under such unpleasant circumstances, I found at this time as on many occasions, that the fire brigade, men and women, were absolutely brilliant. They did a fantastic job under awful conditions and made the task of co-ordinating the three emergency services very much easier. That is exactly what happened at this incident. They carried out a lot of the dirty work and helped me set up a perimeter and reporting area for all the other people who were to arrive. By about 7.30pm, nothing more could be done with the rain still lashing down and it was just a question of guarding the scene of the crash. That would continue all night and it was down to me, until I could be relieved by someone from the night shift.

There I was in the dark, pouring rain, in the woods, soaking wet, hungry and cold, with just human remains for company. Not a happy bunny. That was my lot for what turned out to be the next three hours, until my relief arrived at just past 11.00pm. It was one of those times when I felt that having a drink was well deserved. I found it very sobering sitting at home enjoying my favourite whisky and reflecting on what a difficult day it had been for me, but this paled into insignificance when compared with the tragic outcome suffered by other people.

In November 1975 I was involved in a minor arrest for a simple offence that later had far reaching consequences. On a quiet Sunday morning the details of a car were circulated, the driver had filled up with petrol in Amersham and driven off without paying for it. I took up a position on one of the main roads out of Amersham in the hope that the car would come my way. Well that Sunday, my luck was in! I stopped the car and spoke to the driver. He said that the young lady petrol station attendant, it was not self-service, had put petrol in his car and that he had paid for it. After further questions and not believing that he had paid, I arrested him for theft of petrol; the normal procedure in this situation. The driver was later charged with the theft and bailed to appear at the local Magistrates Court.

Unbeknown to any of us, a barrister had been looking for just such a set of circumstances and he went on to represent the driver at court. His defence was that the allegation was not theft on a technicality. Hearing the explanation, the Magistrates agreed, and the case was thrown out. The effects of such actions at petrol stations, restaurants and shops would have made business difficult to say the least.

The details of such a case can be sent to a higher court to ask for 'a case to be stated' which then becomes case law, in fact a Stated Case. It is quite rare to be involved in such happenings and I asked about the possible outcome. I was told that if the higher court disagreed with the magistrate's decision and we won, then someone high up in the police prosecution set up would have their name as the Stated Case. However, if they agreed and it was not deemed theft and the police 'lost' then the arresting officer, me in this case, would have their name on the case. Well, we lost. It was agreed that it was not theft and the Stated Case of Edwards - v – Ddin of 1976 was set to remain in history. The upshot was that new legislation was required and the Theft Act 1978 was brought in with the new offence of Making Off Without Payment to cover the loophole which had been exposed by my case.

During 1975, there was a string of bomb attacks in London believed to be the work of the IRA. Late one afternoon in October, I was tasked, together with a female police officer, with transporting a female prisoner to Holloway Prison in London. I was allocated a transit van for the trip and the first part of the journey went without a hitch. The prisoner was delivered safely and deposited at the prison. By then it was evening time and we took the 'scenic route' back through London, as my colleague was interested in seeing certain tourist spots.

We had just finished our 'tour' and were heading for the road back to Chesham, travelling along Piccadilly towards Park Lane. We had just passed The Ritz Hotel when there was an almighty explosion, just behind us. There was no doubt that it was a bomb exploding. Being that close, there was no mistaking what we heard and felt. An explosive device had been placed at a bus stop right outside Green Park Underground Station and had detonated seconds after we passed it. I drove a little further down the road, did a U turn and headed back to the scene of the explosion. As I did so a Metropolitan Police officer was running in the same direction, we stopped and picked him up. I parked short of the scene. Getting out of the transit van we found police officers running towards us from every direction. I thought, just for a split second as I got out of the van, that if there was a secondary device then there was absolutely nothing we could do about it. It was a tactic which was sometimes used at that time. We would be caught in the blast.

I saw that someone had been at the bus stop when the bomb was detonated, but there wasn't anything anyone could do for him and a police officer was already there. Such was the preparation and planning of the Met Police, that within no more than two minutes there were dozens of police officers on the scene and more arriving all the time, on foot and in a wide range of vehicles.

They had clearly defined plans which were implemented immediately and out of the chaos, came an impressive police operation. Officers seemed to know their tasks and were getting on with them. Jackie, my policewoman colleague, and I were in Piccadilly near the junction with Bolton Street directing the public away from the scene, when I heard a noise which I at first thought was thunder. It was a loud booming noise and when I looked along Bolton Street there was a mass of people all across the road and running, but towards us, not away. I simply could not understand it. Together with other officers we formed a barrier across the entrance to Piccadilly and turned them round and away from the scene. It reminded me of stampeding cattle in a western film, which have to be turned away from danger.

After that, everything seemed to be so well organised that there was no role for us. I found the senior officer present, reported to him, verified that we were no longer needed and started out for home. Later it was confirmed that a twenty-three-year-old man had died at the bus stop and twenty other people had been injured. The trip back to Chesham was a strange one; neither Jackie nor I spoke on the journey; lost in our own thoughts. Just reflecting on the experience of the past few hours, I realised that if we had passed that bus stop ten seconds later we too would have been victims of the blast.

CHAPTER 3

—

Prepare for Action

"Prepare for action"

T he Support Group was a completely self-contained unit with its own command structure and supervisors. It totalled forty officers and consisted of four parties or shifts of eight constables and one sergeant, overseen by a chief inspector and two inspectors. There was also a constable who dealt with admin. Each party had four unmarked police cars which were crewed by two constables, these were regular crew mates. My car was based at Aylesbury and my new crew mate lived at Oxford and we met up wherever we were working. This could be a different location each day. If there were no major incidents to attend to, then we would go to an area in TVP where we could help out with current problems such as, a spate of burglaries or public disorder; anywhere an extra unit of nine officers in unmarked police cars could assist with local policing. This could be day or night, depending on what the problem was. If necessary, other parties could be summoned too and there could be two, three or four parties working together, thus providing a heavy police presence.

I found that working on this department was wonderful and I settled in very quickly. It was a totally different type of policing. I was now working at Oxford, Reading, Slough and Bletchley, which developed into the new city of Milton Keynes; generally, a different place each day. We were used to support local officers with all sorts of operations, as well as any incident of a major nature. I found out early on that some officers were very wary of us, especially some senior officers who didn't actually like us working in their areas. That is, until something went wrong, or problems occurred where they needed our help.

If there was an especially difficult operation, or assistance was required to gain entry to a drug stronghold or raid premises where a violent response was expected, the Support Group were called upon to take the lead. That is why we were referred to by some as the Heavy Mob. By contrast, there were other colleagues who were extremely keen for us to work alongside them and appreciated our skills and approach. Many of them were interested in joining the department.

However, the primary function of our department was as an armed unit. We dealt with any firearms incident where intelligence or information suggested that firearms would be used or with the illegal use or possession of firearms. After a short time on the department I was allocated a firearms course. All officers on Support Group were supposed to be authorised to carry firearms, but one or two who had failed the course were too good to lose. These officers were allowed to perform ancillary duties such as first aid and as quartermasters, whilst the rest of us were engaged on firearms operations.

The firearms course was of two weeks duration and was in-house, using our own firearms range at Maidenhead. It was a very intensive course; long days and lots of shooting, as well as tactical training. Different scenarios were played out at various locations, indoors as well as out, involving armed incidents which needed to be resolved. The course participants were put under immense pressure during the two weeks, which culminated in a final shooting test on the last day. No matter how well students had done during the week, failure to get the required number of hits on the target on test day, forty six out of fifty, resulted in a failed course. One could also be failed on weapon handling and tactics, so the pressure built up during the two weeks. Stress during the course was nothing compared to that felt on a real firearms job. Being armed in the public arena and having to confront armed criminals, was something else altogether.

The weapons we trained with were .38 Smith and Wesson revolvers and 9mm Browning self-loading pistols. We later upgraded to Glock 17 self-loading pistols and 9mm Heckler and Koch MP5 assault rifles. At the end of the course successful students were authorised to be issued with either of those weapons. I enjoyed the course so much; it was just about the best course I ever attended in the whole of my service. At the end of it, I shot as well on test day as I had done for most of the previous weeks and was hugely relieved to have passed. Phew! I would be able to remain on Support Group. Understandably, for some of the officers who did fail after all their efforts they regarded it as an absolute disaster career wise.

The week after I was authorised to carry firearms for police purposes, we were called out to an incident in an Oxfordshire town. Information was to hand, that a man staying in a second-floor flat was planning to rob a building society that day. It was believed that he was in possession of a sawn off double-barrelled shotgun. We deployed around the flat from 6.00am and quietly and quickly raised the residents either side and had them vacate their homes. We then had a stroke of luck. A girlfriend staying at the flat left for work. When she was a safe distance away, she was detained and questioned regarding the man. What she was able to tell us was very helpful and confirmed that the suspect was inside the flat. We firmed up the armed containment and then started the process of calling him out of the flat.

For a time, there was no answer, but by now we had officers in the flat underneath the target premises and they could hear someone moving about. Eventually our suspect presented himself at the door on the side I was covering. He did exactly as he was told; most people tend to when confronted by a number of armed police officers pointing guns at them. He came out onto the fire escape, down the stairs and was arrested. A search of the flat revealed the double-barrelled shotgun, which he had attempted to hide prior to giving himself up.

The operation went very well and was particularly satisfying for me. This was the first time I had pointed a gun at someone for real, previously it had only been in training. How would I react? I felt a range of emotions from apprehension to excitement but was reassured that I was totally in control. When the potential armed robber came out onto the fire escape, if he had been carrying the shotgun and pointed it at me or any of my colleagues I knew then that I could and would have challenged him and shot him if necessary. When being considered as to the suitability of becoming an authorised firearms officer, one of the questions is, 'Would you be able to shoot someone if it was necessary?' I had considered it for some time before I answered truthfully that I really did not know. Now I knew. After that I was never bothered by that question again. That was the first live operation for me and during the next five and a half years I spent on

Support Group as a constable, I was involved in many firearms operations. This first incident gave me the confidence to continue as an effective and reliable firearms officer.

LEGAL AND GENERAL MURDER TRIAL AT THE OLD BAILEY

During the middle of 1977, a murder trial at the Old Bailey came to an end when a number of people were convicted of murder and other offences. The court had heard details about the torture and killing of what were described as two small time crooks. The body of one, with head and hands missing had been found floating down the River Thames and the other was shot and killed whilst trying to find the first one. Those convicted were accused of being part of the London gang known as Legal and General. The trial lasted for seven months and at the time, was the longest criminal trial in Old Bailey history. The police officer leading the enquiry was the legendary gangbuster, Commander Bert Wickstead.

We in Support Group became involved the previous December, when a convicted criminal had been declared a supergrass; someone in custody for serious crimes allowed to do a deal on his offences if he agreed to give evidence against other criminals. This supergrass had been in prison awaiting his own trial when he was 'banged up' (meaning he shared a cell) with others awaiting different trials. He had already agreed to give evidence against members of his own gang. He was then locked up with at least one member of the Legal and General gang. He alleged that he had been party to conversations where they had described the killings.

The supergrass was thought to be at risk, so he was kept in custody in the TVP area and was taken to the Old Bailey each day to give his evidence. The first morning we took him to court we assembled at Windsor police station and were met by the Metropolitan Police Special Escort Group (SEG), a double crewed marked police vehicle. Our part of the convoy consisted of three Support Group cars, unmarked except for stick on blue lights as well as a marked TVP traffic car bringing up the rear. Owing to the perceived risk to the supergrass, all Support Group officers were armed. He was in the middle unmarked car. I was driving the lead Support Group vehicle immediately behind the Met police car. We were briefed by the Met officers who specialised in this type of convoy. The rule for an operation of this type is that the wheels of the police vehicles do not stop for any reason. We were to travel on the M4 motorway for part of the journey and then follow a pre-arranged route into the Old Bailey. Preparing to depart, the driver of the lead car said to me, 'All you have to do is follow me, if my car goes through any gap then so will yours and all the others'. Sounded good to me.

We set off at 8.00am and it was 'blues and twos', blue lights and two tone horns, all the way. The first part of the journey went without any problems; the convoy was working well and very tight. As we neared London a car to car radio message told us that the M4 ahead was blocked by an accident, so we came off and took to the A4.

A short time later I could see the traffic in front was at a total standstill and the road appeared to be blocked. The lead car radioed to say that there was a very wide grass verge and footpath ahead and we were going to take that to get around the blockage. Luckily there weren't any pedestrians as we sped along the path. No problems there and we were away again.

As we entered London the Met police motorcyclists did a fantastic job, riding ahead blocking each roundabout and major junction and we sailed through the traffic. They then shot past the convoy and did the same at the next junction. The radio told us that, as we were going through Kensington the traffic had been stopped and we were to take to the offside of the road. 8.20am driving past Harrods, 60 miles an hour, wrong side of the road; it's the only way to travel!

Before much longer we were at the back door of the Old Bailey and the first part of our task was complete. There was one minor mishap on arrival. As we were deploying out of the police vehicles, one of the officer's handgun slipped out of its holster and skidded across the pavement! Thankfully, no harm done but I must remember to take the mickey out of Trumps when I see him next. We stayed with our supergrass for the entire time including being deployed in Court Number One whilst he was giving evidence. This whole procedure took place over the course of the next few days, with the same format for travelling back to the TVP area. The only difference was that in the afternoon at the end of the day's court activities, the Met police lead car crew asked how long the journey had taken in the morning, purely for operational reasons of course. It had nothing to do with them wanting to beat the time taken by their mates in the morning. The fastest time of all was recorded at 38 minutes, Windsor to the Old Bailey!

One day returning to Windsor around 4.30pm, we were almost out of London and going well when we were held up in the outside lane of the elevated section of the M4. When I say held up, I mean we had slowed to approximately 60 mph owing to heavy traffic in all three lanes. The marked traffic car at the front was doing an excellent job clearing the traffic in lane three for us to have a clear run, until they came up behind a black cab. For some reason the cab driver did not see or chose not to see the police car behind him with headlights on full, blue lights everywhere and two tones going full blast.

This went on for about a mile or so, all the other traffic was diving out of the way but not the black cab. I was just behind the traffic car and could see the officer in the front passenger seat going spare. Eventually the cab driver must have looked in his rear-view mirror and seen the police car and blue lights almost buried in the back of his cab. He almost left the road trying to get out of the way and into lane two. The traffic car pulled alongside the cab, held its position whilst the officer in the front passenger seat half climbed out of the window. I mean the top half of him, waist up, was out of the window giving the cab driver some verbals. He was giving him such a gob full that I could hear him shouting from my car behind and all this at 60 mph in lane three of the M4. Fantastic!

On arriving back at Windsor and putting our supergrass away safely, we always took the Met crew for a cup of tea. I told the officer, who had been doing the Superman impression of nearly flying, how impressive it had looked when he 'advised the cab driver about the standard of his driving'. He said that not only had he given him advice but he had reported him for a traffic offence at the same time. Wow. I would love to have been in Court when that one came up and heard the circumstances relayed to the Magistrates.

One particular day we were waiting in the court annexe to be called in, surrounding and protecting the supergrass, when two familiar figures approached to see what was going on. It was close to Christmas and it transpired that these two people had been the guests of the Old Bailey judges for their Christmas lunch. It was Morecombe and Wise. Eric said to us that he had just seen Jack Reagan (of the TV series The Sweeney, very popular at the time) and that Jack had told us to carry on doing a good job.

Christmas was approaching fast and at fairly short notice we were informed that our involvement with the supergrass was to finish. He had completed giving his evidence in this trial at the Old Bailey and was to be taken elsewhere. Under these circumstances what happens next is on a need to know basis and we didn't need to know. He was handed over to officers from another police force and would eventually be taken to start his term of imprisonment.

The whole experience of the fast runs to and from London and being in Court One at the Old Bailey was an extremely interesting experience and something new for us all.

CHAPTER 4

—

Guardian of the Peace

Guardian of the peace

Two parties of Support Group were directed to a disused army base for specialised training on a specific incident of which we had no prior knowledge. We were informed that the Commonwealth Heads of Government Meeting, which takes place every four years, was being held in London between 8th and 15th June 1977. It came as no surprise, to be told that all Heads of the Commonwealth Governments were invited, the clue is in the title isn't it and almost without exception they always all attended. A potential problem had arisen when information was received that the President of Uganda, Idi Amin, had declared his intention to attend. He had not been invited because of accusations and allegations made against him about his long term tyrannical rule over his people. He was a ruthless dictator. It was alleged that political opponents and countless numbers of his people had disappeared or had been subjected to unspeakable atrocities. It was always accepted that if the situation ever arose where he was 'on offer' outside Uganda, he would be arrested for the alleged crimes.

It was believed that it was his intention to attend the London conference. We were made aware that his plane would be directed to a military airfield in the TVP area, where he and his entourage would be met by us. We were to be armed and it was our role to disarm his personal bodyguards, who always travelled with him wherever he went. At that time, a senior Home Office official would inform him that he was being detained. Yeah right, as simple as that. We made the point early on that we felt sure that his personal bodyguards would not surrender their weapons just because we asked them to. We were to be supported by specialist military personnel from elsewhere, experts in their field, who would give us the right level of support and assistance.

We started training. We had some of our own people playing the part of Idi Amin and his bodyguards and we trained for all sorts of different scenarios. We trained all week, the first two days being absolute chaos. On day one, it ended with three or four of us, sometimes the Home Office official and on most occasions all of his bodyguards, being shot! We trained with pyrotechnics to assist and cause a diversion. That worked well and helped, but had its lighter moments. One of our team threw a thunder flash to simulate a stun grenade at the optimum time, but in training he didn't throw it far enough, it landed at the feet of one of our sergeants and blew the toe cap off his boot! By the end of the week we felt a little more confident about the possible outcome, although it was still fraught with danger.

It's important to remember that this was a time when mobile phones and pagers were still relatively new technology. The whole team was issued with freshly delivered pagers to keep us informed of events. In the days leading up to the conference it was widely reported in the press and news outlets; both The Sun and The Times carried the detailed story, that Idi Amin was intent on coming to London. There was intense speculation about the possible outcome. Come the day, we were on standby awaiting orders, when my pager went off with instructions to contact Police HQ. We were all informed that Idi Amin had indeed taken off in his plane and a flight plan had been lodged for a journey to London. We were to rendezvous at our pre-arranged location at the airfield and prepare for the plane's arrival. So that was it, now it was for real.

Driving to the location I was going over the plan in my mind, ticking off the various possible scenarios, wondering what the outcome might be. Before our arrival, we were told over the police radio to stand down and return to HQ. We were informed that Idi Amin's plane had been in the air, flown around for some time, before returning to Entebbe without ever leaving Ugandan air space. It is fair to say that we were very much relieved. It would have been interesting but also extremely difficult, if not impossible to effect his arrest and detention without injuries or fatalities. I am still convinced that it had the potential for disaster.

In order to comply with classified events, nothing much was reported. Suffice it to say that he didn't turn up and that was the last heard on the subject. I now find that under the thirty years rule the documents relating to this event have become declassified and can be recounted. I was surprised in 2007 to discover that thirty years on, it was reported in the following terms;

(Newspaper headline) 'Declassified documents reveal the British plotted to assassinate Idi Amin at CHOGM'.

'Previously classified British government documents reveal that Idi Amin and his entourage would have been shot at any airport in Britain if Amin had attended the Commonwealth Heads of Government Meeting (CHOGM) in 1977. Field Marshall Idi Amin has been dead for over three years but he is still a controversial figure. Had Amin, the ruthless Ugandan dictator insisted on coming to Britain in 1977, he would have been assassinated.

I am merely quoting here from the report of the declassified document but feel that I must take issue with use of the word 'assassinated'. This suggests unlawful killing or execution and in purist terms means murder. The whole purpose was to detain Idi Amin and his bodyguards who were expected to be heavily armed. It was never the intention for him to be killed but it may have been the likely outcome.

NORTH ASTON SIEGE

Early one summer morning in 1978, two parties of Support Group were directed to an armed siege at a small village in Oxfordshire called North Aston. Just before midnight the previous evening a local man, who had earlier abducted his five-year-old son from a safe house, burst his way into the cottage occupied by a farm manager and his girlfriend. The man, who was being sought by police, made threats to the couple and barricaded himself, his son and the girlfriend in a first-floor bedroom. He found a double-barrelled shotgun and cartridges belonging to the farm manager, who raised the alarm. By the time we arrived the siege was well under way, with the man and his hostages occupying the front bedroom of a lovely old stone cottage overlooking the village green. Contact had been made with him, he was demanding an inquiry into allegations he was making against a police officer from nearby Banbury.

By mid-afternoon on this, day one of the siege, it appeared that this operation may have legs and that it was not going to be solved anytime soon. Contingency plans evolved whereby the two parties of Support Group, fulfilling our main function as the Tactical Firearms Team would perform rolling twelve hour duties. 0600 – 1800 hours at the scene on days. We would be relieved by the other two parties who would perform duty from 1800 – 0600 hours on nights and that arrangement would remain until the problem was resolved.

We soon settled into a routine, police negotiators had made contact with the man and dialogue was taking place. My role, together with my colleagues, was as first responder to make an armed entry into the bedroom, should it become necessary. To that end we were ensconced in the downstairs front-room, standing by at the foot of the stairs. The whole house had by now been taken over by the police.

There were various highs and lows, negotiations were breaking down, the man would make threats, clearly brandish the loaded shotgun and so we prepared to force an entry into the bedroom. Just as quickly, he would calm down and we would stand down. On day two the young lady, held hostage since the start, was allowed to leave the cottage. The siege continued with concern for the five-year-old boy still being held hostage by his father.

Our routine was well set by now. Our technical staff had installed a bank of cameras permanently monitored from the downstairs front room, giving us a vitally important overall picture of events. We also made use of everyone on the team, even those not authorised to carry firearms. These colleagues performed a number of duties, not least the very important one of a constant supply of tea and coffee for the rest of us. One such officer on the team was Dave, a PC who was invaluable, an absolute diamond who carried out a multitude of tasks, but he also had a reputation of sometimes putting his foot in it. One morning about day three, the negotiators had been involved in a session attempting to persuade the man to give up peacefully and we were watching him on the cameras, judging his reaction. Suddenly the screens went blank in sequence one after the other, one, two, three, four, five, all blank. Twiddling the knobs and even banging the screens had no effect; they just stared back at us. An urgent call went out to the technicians to attend and sort out the problem. At that point our colleague Dave, brought a tray of tea and coffee, enough for everyone, from where he had been busying himself in the kitchen at the back of the cottage. Another colleague congratulated him on the much needed refreshments especially as there was a shortage of usable power points to boil the kettle. "That's no problem," he said. "I just took out a plug which didn't seem to be connected to anything"...Yes, it had to be. He had unplugged the main power connection to the screens, that's why they went blank. We swiftly plugged it back in and were immediately up and running again.

Later that day, came a crucial point in attempting to resolve the situation peaceably and without harm to anyone. One condition from the man was that he wanted publicity for his demand for an inquiry. To that end he had prepared a statement, which he wanted printed in the local newspaper. He said that if it was published he would consider giving up and coming out. The local paper was contacted and agreed to print four special copies of their paper to include the prepared statement. It was very restricted so that one copy would be sent into the bedroom for the man, one for the negotiator so that he could see what the man was referring to, one for the officer in charge of the control room and one for the Chief Constable, so that he was fully up to speed with events. In the afternoon the four special copies of the newspaper were delivered and distributed.

A short time later the man wanted to discuss the details of his statement in the paper and asked to speak to the negotiator. A problem arose immediately when the negotiator went to retrieve his copy, which he had placed next to the screens, and discovered that it wasn't there. A search revealed nothing, and the other copies had been delivered to where they needed to be. A minor panic was averted when our tea making colleague Dave appeared and someone noticed that he had a newspaper sticking out of the back pocket of his uniform trousers. He said that the announcement was due that afternoon about the proposed increase in police pay and he had listened to it away from the house in a nearby police portacabin. He added that when we were ready, he would go through it for us as he had written the new pay rates across the newspaper he had found lying about near the screens. The paper was taken from him and on checking, yes indeed it was 'THE one' we were looking for, but now it had our new pay rates scrawled all over the front page. Cue for the negotiator to throw toys from pram and to ban our hero from ever setting foot in that cottage again, ever, ever, ever. Phew, problem solved.

There was one more memorable event before the whole operation reached its conclusion. Each morning when we arrived on site to relieve our colleagues from their tour of night duty, we spent some time with them catching up on the current situation and what had occurred in the twelve hours we had been away. This was always very professional and precise, but with our inter-party rivalry it always degenerated into friendly humorous banter. 'It's alright leave it to us boys, we will resolve it before you get back here,' etc… Then we got down to our duties for the day. On the morning of day five our normal question of, "Much happen during the night?" was met with lack of eye contact and vague answers. Clearly something had happened in the twelve hours we had been away. The siege was still on and the man was apparently asleep. Once alone with our firearms team colleagues, they told us what had happened. During the previous evening the negotiations appeared to be going well, the man was clearly indicating that he was not looking forward to another night barricaded in the bedroom. It had reached a point where, 'negotiations were at a delicate stage.' The main negotiator was hopeful that he had just about persuaded the man to throw the shotgun out of the bedroom window and come out with his son. There was a lull in the proceedings and a break for the man to reflect on the offer and consider the next move.

One of the main observation and armed containment points was from behind a massive old oak tree on the edge of the village green, directly in front of the cottage and a few yards from the front bedroom window. The officer behind the tree had been in position for some time and was aware that nothing seemed to be happening, so to help move things along he was heard to call out, "You in the house, its okay you can come out now, we give up!" Unfortunately, this did not have the desired effect. In fact it had quite the opposite. The man was not a happy bunny and he reloaded the shotgun, which he had previously unloaded. He came to the window and shouted threats at the officer behind the tree making everyone aware in no uncertain terms that he wasn't coming out under any circumstances. It appeared that the negotiator was slightly upset too, so the message was to tread carefully for a little while as things were somewhat fragile.

During the course of the morning there was a real push from the negotiators and eventually the man agreed to give up. He broke the now unloaded shotgun open, dropped it out of the front bedroom window and came out under instructions, carrying his son in his arms. In some respects, we were slightly disappointed that he chose that day to give up. The next day was the start of three rest days for us and to work on those with such long hours would have been financially beneficial! There is no truth in the rumour circulating at the time, that we tried to persuade him to stay in there for another three days!

However, the main objective had been achieved, the situation had been peacefully resolved, with no shots fired, no-one injured and all the hostages and the hostage taker safe and well. It had taken five days and fourteen hours, a major inconvenience for the village but worth it all in the end.

CHAPTER 5

—

Football Hooliganism

Rushing the goal keeper

During the middle and late '70s and '80s football hooliganism in the UK was at its height. The two main football teams in the TVP area, Oxford United and Reading FC, had their moments. Oxford United in particular saw some time in the then top division of football, the First Division. We on Support Group, were asked to perform a specialist public order role at all matches where the potential for problems was evident. At some really special local derby matches, there was always the potential for major disorder. Any matches featuring Oxford or Reading playing against Portsmouth or Swindon or playing against each other, were always heavily policed. In addition, while Oxford United were in the top flight they played against several teams whose supporters had a reputation for causing trouble.

Reading was drawn at home to play First Division side, Southampton FC, in what was then the League Cup. The intelligence from the Southampton police was that there was lots of trouble anticipated and they were correct. More than three hundred police were on duty for this match. Our normal role was to patrol in our plain cars in the vicinity of the ground, looking for potential trouble spots until kick off and then deploy where required, inside the ground.

At this match all of Support Group were called into the ground thirty minutes before kick-off, because of problems on the terraces. This was before the advent of all-seater stadiums. We were sent into the away supporters open terrace, where Reading and Southampton supporters had entered the same stand. Several fights had already taken place. Ball bearings had been thrown or fired from catapults. One of the tactics of the hooligan element was to try and float urine filled balloons above the opposing supporters or police and pierce them by throwing darts.

The two lots of supporters were separated only by a chain link fence and were intent on getting at each other by any means. After a semblance of order had been achieved, we retreated to the pitch perimeter. We were facing the opposing factions so that we could make sorties into the middle of them when the need arose, which it did several times. We climbed the fence in front of us and forced our way onto the terraces and a number of arrests were made after the crowd surged in an effort to reach opposing fans.

We assisted the arresting officers getting their prisoners out of the crowd and at the same time watched their backs. This was a real battle to protect our colleagues as the whole crowd seemed intent on attempting to release those who had been arrested, as well as trying to assault us. We reached the relative safety of the edge of the pitch. As we were pushing the crowd back, one of them right in front of me pointed behind me and shouted, "Look at that, the bastards have pulled his leg off!"

What a stupid prat, I thought. As the crowd retreated I turned, checked behind me and sure enough, there was one of our sergeants running down the touchline with a leg! Its owner having been arrested was being taken away. It transpired that the prisoner had a false leg and had struggled so much during the arrest that it had come off. As he was led away he continued to cause trouble by spitting at the opposing fans. What a photograph that made for the local press.

The following Easter we had a really busy weekend of football. On Good Friday Reading were at home to Portsmouth, where we made sixty nine arrests. Easter Monday brought Aldershot, then top of the table, to Reading and a further sixty two arrests, a total of one hundred and thirty one for the two matches over the four days. Oh by the way, sandwiched in between was the Saturday match at Oxford, a small matter of Oxford United versus Swindon. This local derby is always a battle and another basket full of arrests were made there as well. The following season Oxford entertained Millwall FC, which brought its own problems. In later seasons, Birmingham City and Leeds United proved especially difficult in policing terms.

Having spent some time dealing with so called football hooligans, I found it interesting, once everything had quietened down, to talk to them about what they were doing and why. At one Oxford United match, there had been a good deal of missiles thrown by hard core Oxford supporters from the back of the stand behind the goal on the home supporter's terrace. We were tasked with identifying the offenders and, making our way into the stand, arresting and removing them. Not as simple as it sounds. We went in mob handed, singled out our targets to be arrested and then the difficult bit, fighting our way out with the prisoners.

When we reached our objective, I took hold of one young man who at first, didn't even seem to realise who I was and that he was being arrested. He was shouting abuse having just thrown a missile and when I took hold of him, I saw his eyes were glazed, he was clearly on some sort of high. By now, there were a number of away supporters who had infiltrated the home terrace and fights were breaking out all around us. Those of us with prisoners, eventually removed them from the stand with the help of our colleagues and crewmates who were protecting our backs.

We took our prisoners to the police detention area, a mini police station behind the main stand. Away from the stand my prisoner quietened down and I told him again that he had been arrested and the reason. Whilst we were waiting to be processed I got chatting to him, unlike a lot of prisoners in those circumstances who act Jack the lad, he was very quiet and subdued. He was not under the influence of drink or drugs as I had first thought. He told me that he had nothing much in his life, no family, no job, and no real friends. He lived alone in one pokey room in a rundown area of Oxford and had no prospects. Every week at the football, home and away when he could afford it, he was part of a huge gang who worked together to try and attack the opposition supporters. They were all his so called 'friends' and all he had to do to gain acceptance, was to join in. It was easy to understand where he was coming from, he had nothing else in his life but once a week for the whole of the football season, he was part of something and felt that he belonged. It was very difficult to try and dissuade him from the path that he was on.

CHAPTER 6

—

Famous or Infamous

"Salvation"

orking in the TVP area it was inevitable that I would come across celebrities and people of note. It has been an absolute delight for me to meet a whole variety of famous people: politicians, actors, TV stars, footballers and a magician!

POLITICAL FIGURES

I have mentioned previously my involvement with Lord Carrington and Prime Ministers, Edward Heath and Harold Wilson. It has been a fascinating experience to be involved with the security of a total of six British PMs. In addition to those two, there was James Callaghan, Margaret Thatcher, John Major and Tony Blair, when they were each in residence at the Prime Minister's country home, Chequers.

James Callaghan was Prime Minister from 1976 to 1979. During his time there were many visiting dignitaries to Chequers who required extra armed security. One such visitor in 1977, was the newly elected Prime Minister of Israel, Menachem Begin. I was one of the officers in close proximity to the main house of Chequers when his convoy arrived. For the press call of photographs, the PM asked for two police officers to stand with him and Mr Begin. As my crewmate and I were closest, we were press ganged into standing on the front steps either side of the two Prime Ministers. I particularly remember this because Mr Begin was not very tall and Mr Callaghan had awful dandruff!

There were many times when officers from my specialist department were required to boost the security at Chequers. This was especially so during Margaret Thatcher's time as Prime Minister, 1979 to 1990. Without doubt the most difficult and emotional time was in October 1984. The IRA had placed an explosive device at The Grand Hotel in Brighton during the Conservative Party Conference. As a result of the explosion, five people were killed and thirty-four were injured, some seriously, but Mrs Thatcher escaped unharmed. The statement from the IRA included the chilling phrase, 'Today we were unlucky but remember we only have to be lucky once: you will have to be lucky always.'

The security at Chequers was immediately reviewed and armed patrols were increased for the weekend following the end of the conference. I was a sergeant on Support Group by now, the primary function of the department being the Tactical Firearms Team. My team were on day shifts for that weekend. On the Sunday morning, I was informed that the Prime Minister was coming out into the grounds with the intention of going for a walk. The grounds of Chequers are huge. From a security perspective this can present difficulties, not least because of a public footpath which crosses the main drive. I deployed my officers at various strategic points to cover wherever Mrs Thatcher was likely to be walking. She came out of the house and approached me. She said that she was aware of my responsibilities for her safety, but she really felt the need for a walk in the fresh air and would appreciate some space if that was possible. What a quandary; trying to get the balance just right. Not surprisingly the PM had the answer. She asked if it would be alright if she went for her walk with the dog, indicating to the German shepherd police dog and handler nearby. And that was that, she was off, saying, 'Come on then.'

I am not sure if it was the dog or the handler she was talking to but off they went, with my team trying to monitor her from a distance to give her the space she craved. I was so impressed by her resolve, as only a few days previously personal friends had died and others were severely injured. It was no surprise that she was upset after enduring such a traumatic and tragic event, but still showed a steeliness for which she was renowned.

My team had another interesting encounter with Mrs Thatcher over Christmas 1985. With the extra security still in place, the thorny question came up of who was going to work the day shift on 25th December. Lots were drawn to see which of the four teams would work Christmas Day. By now we were working twelve hour shifts, 0600 – 1800 hours. My party lost and that meant working on the one day we all hoped not to.

However, in an attempt to make the day as Christmassy as possible one of the team, Noel and his wife, who lived in nearby Aylesbury, volunteered to replicate their family Christmas dinner and cook one for the whole team. On Christmas morning the patrol rota was arranged so that Noel could collect the turkey and all the trimmings and bring it to the police post within the grounds. It was then his job to finish the cooking and serve the dinners to our team in rotation. This was done when they came in from their patrols within the grounds. It was magnificent, we had a wonderful meal with Christmas pudding to follow and even had poppers and crackers and all served beautifully by Noel wearing his Union Jack apron.

By mid afternoon we had just finished, when there was a call from the main house telling me that Mrs Thatcher and family and her guests were on their way to the police post to wish us a Happy Christmas. Slightly panicky, we rushed to clear everything away but before we had finished, the PM and her party were at the door. We invited them in and I explained that we also had been having Christmas dinner. Mrs Thatcher had brought a huge Christmas cake for us and Denis, her husband, several bottles of drink, for when we were off duty of course. All Carol Thatcher, her daughter, wanted to do was take lots of photos, having grabbed our camera with which we had been recording our jolly celebration. Mrs Thatcher insisted on having a photograph taken with, 'her police officers.' The photograph of my team with the PM, has the unusual sight of Noel still wearing his Union Jack pinny and paper hat, whilst fulfilling the important task of providing armed protection for her. A good time was had by all, a truly unforgettable experience.

All of my dealings with Mrs Thatcher and her family were excellent, with no problems at all. Denis was an absolute diamond, he was forever out on the grass at the front of the rose garden with a golf club and ball practising his shots.

John Major and his wife were very pleasant in all dealings, but we did not see as much of them at Chequers as we had previous Prime Ministers.

Tony Blair was Prime Minister for ten years. The unusual feature of his tenure as PM was that he had a young family, which sometimes gave a different dimension to the security operation. This could include some of the protection team being asked to play football with the youngsters. What an ideal opportunity to kick the Prime Minister without any repercussions.

I was also involved with the security of three Presidents of the United States, two serving and one former. President Ronald Reagan visited during Mrs Thatcher's time as Prime Minister and whilst Tony Blair was PM President Bill Clinton also stayed at Chequers. It was fascinating to see the American Secret Service way of protecting the President in comparison with our own procedures in the UK. While President Clinton was at Chequers, he visited a local golf club and played two holes. The security operation for that was immense.

I was aware that when he visited another part of the UK, he called in at a pub and had a pint of good old English ale. There was always an advance party ahead of the President and a follow up party once he had left. The follow up party took possession of the pint glass he had drunk from and smashed it. The reason given was so that his fingerprints could not be taken from the glass where he had held it and his DNA could not be obtained.

In 1978, the former President, Richard Nixon appeared at Oxford University, accepting an invitation to speak at the Oxford Union. Getting him in was a challenge, as a large crowd of students tried to prevent him entering the building, screaming abuse and trying to pelt him with eggs. Nevertheless, he was able to take part in a ninety-minute question and answer session. Our task was to then get him out. The problem with security for speakers at the Oxford Union, is that the only way in and out is via a small one way side street, and everyone knows that. When the ex-President was due to depart there were several hundred people, mostly students, who appeared desperate to get close enough to cause him some grief. Fortunately, we thwarted their efforts. We were able to get him into his vehicle and get it away, with nothing more than a few wild kicks at the car. A new group had been formed to organise the mob who tried to disrupt the visit. It was called CREEP, the Campaign to Resist the Efforts of the Ex-President! Nice one.

One of the saddest duties I performed relating to a politician was in April 1979 at the funeral of MP Airey Neave, the Shadow Northern Ireland Secretary. He was killed in his car at the House of Commons by a bomb attached to the vehicle. It was believed to be the work of the Irish National Liberation Army. (INLA). The funeral took place at his small, quiet home village of Longworth, Berkshire. He had died the week before and clearly the security for the funeral was a major concern. Under such circumstances it is extremely difficult for all involved, not least the family, friends and colleagues. To have a total 'lock down' where nothing and nobody moves without intrusive searches, is not acceptable. As always, we were looking to achieve a balance, where the family could be allowed to grieve, and the funeral be conducted without hordes of police officers being visible. We aimed to accomplish this while at the same time maintaining security for everyone, especially with a number of people attending who were at risk of being attacked. I am confident that on this occasion we struck that balance.

Much later in my career, I was superintendent in charge of Operations at police headquarters and was due to take up this new post on a Monday. I was asked to meet the then Home Secretary, Jack Straw, at his home on Sunday, the day before I actually started my new role. I was aware that he wanted to ask questions about his security. I travelled out to see him and his wife at their country home to discuss the matter. He did make a request to which I had to say no. It was only after I left and was returning home that the significance struck me, I had just had to say 'no' to the Home Secretary and refuse his request and I hadn't even started my new job yet!

SPORTS STARS

I have been very fortunate to meet some of my sporting heroes. As a sergeant on Support Group, I was travelling back to my home station with my crew mate Noel having finished an operation. We were on the Marlow Bypass in our normal unmarked police vehicle. As we overtook one particular car, I looked at the driver and told Noel to pull in front and stop the car. He said, "What has he done? I didn't see anything."

I said, "It doesn't matter, just pull him in." Our unmarked car had a pop up sign on the rear parcel shelf which when activated, lit up with 'Police –Stop'. We switched on the sign and Noel brought the police vehicle to a halt in front of the car that interested me. I went to speak to the driver. Noel followed me a few seconds later to the driver's side of the car. I should now point out that I am a huge football supporter, especially Manchester United, Noel is not but he is aware of me being a big sports fan.

As he arrived at the car and saw who I was talking to, he said, "Oh no, I thought it was something important."

I pointed out that it doesn't get much more important than this. The driver was one of my all-time heroes, George Best. George was very happy to talk football for just a few brief minutes. Now knowing of his later transgressions, he was probably relieved that it was something as simple as an adoring fan after an autograph. He was very pleasant, looked very good considering that the main part of his footballing career was over and was so charming that even Noel thought he was pretty cool. He was after all, one of the greatest footballers who ever played the game and it was a delight for me to have met him.

Some years later I became a football coach with a local boy's football club, Chiltern Athletic. Both of my sons played for the club. Through my work I became aware that the

Bobby Charlton Soccer School was then sponsored by the Trustee Savings Bank. Through our local branch I arranged for the Soccer School to be hosted by our football club. Our base was at a local school and arrangements were made for the great man himself to come and meet the children and publicise the Soccer School. I was now a local police inspector and the organisers thought it would be good for me to be there too. So, the event was put in place and that was my first meeting with the true legend and hero.

Some weeks later, the Soccer School came to town and I wondered if some of the younger children who had signed up would know who Bobby Charlton was. By now he was about 60 years of age. I need not have worried. It was quite normal to see all the dads talking to him and asking their questions. He had such charisma and at one point I saw him talking to a group of ten-year olds; they were sitting round him in a big circle and hanging on his every word. I also had the opportunity to talk to him and asked: How good was George Best? How good an England Manager would Brian Clough have been? Who was the best player he ever played with or against?

The different age groups always completed their training by playing a match. I saw Bobby go round all the groups and take part in the games. I was involved in coaching an under sixteen's team and when he came to my group, he joined in our match. At one point he passed the ball to me! No, just let me absorb that for a moment, BOBBY CHARLTON PASSED THE BALL TO ME! My life was now complete, I just wanted to pick the ball up and go home. Later, when I arrived at our house I was in a bit of daze. My wife asked me how it had gone and all I can remember saying is, "Bobby Charlton passed to me." I must say that he was an absolute star: the kids loved him, the parents loved him. He always had time to stop and talk to everyone. He stayed and took part in the whole two days of the Soccer School. The man is a legend and a true gentleman.

I was watching the 1995 football international, Republic of Ireland versus England, on TV when the game was abandoned owing to crowd problems and football hooliganism. In the 22nd minute Ireland scored to take the lead. Almost immediately, some England supporters sitting in the stands above the Irish fans began pelting them with missiles. Plastic seats and bits of iron rained down on the Irish fans, some with small children. Debris landed on the pitch and the match could not continue. The players were led to the safety of the dressing rooms and in the 27th minute the match was abandoned, but the violence persisted. It was apparent to me, seeing the looks on the player's faces, that they had not experienced anything like that at close hand before. Some looked quite shocked and bewildered by the experience. I had been involved in dealing with football hooliganism during the bad times of the '80s and in a mad moment, I wrote to the Football Association (FA) giving my impressions of what I had just seen on TV. I related some of my experiences and gave my opinion; something should be done to educate the players about the hooligan element which attaches itself to football.

A couple of weeks later, I received a telephone call from David Davies of the FA thanking me for my letter and agreeing that something should be done. So, what was I going to do about it? I offered to do a presentation to the England players about football hooliganism, one which I had delivered a number of times before. Previously while I was serving at High Wycombe, I delivered the talk to Martin O'Neill, the manager, and players and staff at Wycombe Wanderers, who were then moving their way up in the football world.

David Davis accepted my offer. He asked me if I would be prepared to go to FA headquarters at Lancaster Gate, London and show the presentation to him and the England Manager, Terry Venables. Would I be prepared to visit FA HQ, the hallowed halls and meet with the England football manager? Was he for real? Well I needed to think about that for a second. Okay, I thought about it and yes of course I would do it. Who wouldn't?

It was all arranged and a few weeks later I found myself at Football HQ. I spent about an hour with Terry Venables and David Davies, showing them the content of the presentation. At the end it is correct to say that Terry Venables loved it and wanted it for the England squad, but David Davies didn't like it. He was concerned about showing the players some of the weapons and tactics used by so called football fans. It was intriguing to witness their discussion. I was then thanked and told that it would be discussed further and that I would be contacted. I drove away thinking that was it, I would hear no more but at least I had enjoyed the experience and I had met Terry Venables, a charismatic person, I liked him a lot. It was a memorable event and was very well received.

Much to my surprise I received a call a few days later asking me to attend the next gathering of the England football squad to deliver the presentation. WOW!

Later that year the England squad had assembled at their hotel in Burnham Beeches, which happens to be in the Thames Valley Police area, prior to a match at Wembley. I had been allocated a one-hour afternoon slot to deliver my presentation. I was met by Terry Venables and David Platt, the current England captain, who took me to where the England squad were gathered with the coaching staff. How lucky was I, it was fantastic to stand in front of such a star studded group and speak to them. As part of the talk to demonstrate a particular point, I threw an apple into the audience. I picked out David Seaman, the England goalkeeper, and threw it to him. Although he fumbled it and took some stick from the other players, he did catch it. The next thing I saw was Paul Gascoigne, Gazza to everyone, lying on the floor in front of all the other players, munching away on my apple. Fortunately, I had a couple more with me.

I used the apple to show the violent ingenuity of some football hooligans. During a match an apple would be thrown from within one of the stands towards the opposing supporters terraces and several hands would go up to catch it. This was repeated with a second and perhaps a third apple. By now more supporters were interested and made a grab for it. The next one to be thrown had six or seven craft knife blades half inserted into the apple. This converted it into a horrendous weapon. It was then thrown, following the path of the previous apples, to be caught by the unsuspecting fans. I showed the apple with blades to the players, but needless to say I didn't throw it. David Seaman would have definitely dropped that one.

The talk ended with a video of football hooligans in action. I explained that I had a couple of other videos, but that was all we had time for. Terry Venables summed up by saying a few words about these problems within football. I was then presented with an FA fountain pen and given a resounding round of applause by the squad. It felt quite surreal and I enjoyed it immensely, I think the players and coaching staff did too. As I was packing things away, several players came by to look at the weapons I had displayed and to say thank you. The manager had already announced that the squad had the rest of the afternoon off. Some of the players asked me if I had to leave then or could I spare the time to show the other videos I had mentioned. Could I? What do you think? I put the videos on to play and sat with the players and answered questions as we went along. I was sitting with Gary Neville who was new to the England squad, Gary Pallister, Andy Cole, all of Manchester United and other England players including Alan Shearer, John Barnes and Peter Beardsley. It doesn't get much better than this.

All too soon it was time to leave. After saying my farewells, I was in the car driving away reflecting on one of the most amazing, unforgettable experiences. Some years later, on reading Terry Venable's autobiography there was a passage in his book referring to that day and me delivering the presentation. It reminded me of how much I enjoyed a magical afternoon with the England football squad.

OTHER CELEBRITIES

When writing this book and with the benefit of hindsight I was unsure whether to include the following anecdote. However, having met with and written about murderers, rapists, paedophiles, armed robbers and countless other criminals I decided on balance to include it.

The annual street fair at Amersham always caused problems, the main High Street being closed to traffic for about four days with diversions and the inevitable hold ups. In those days to help with the difficulties, it always seemed like a good idea to have a police officer controlling the traffic. If you didn't have any hold ups and traffic chaos before the police arrived, you sure as hell did once they started doing what was called 'Point Duty'! With only a few months service, I was doing a sterling job near the junction of the two main roads approaching the diversion for the fair. I was putting into good practice the specific training I had received for controlling traffic, plus a few of my own improvisations. Whenever it was time to stop the flow of traffic in one direction to give the other end a go, I would select which car I was going to stop, stand full on and point at the driver before raising my hand in a perfectly executed 'STOP' hand signal.

I had been doing this to great effect for about two hours, when I chose to stop a bright red E Type Jaguar. Well you would wouldn't you? If for no other reason than to admire it whilst it was stationary nearby. As the car slowed and came to a halt, the driver leant forward and from behind the windscreen pointed back at me in an exaggerated manner. Being engaged on point duty for two hours solid can be quite tiring and the last thing you want is some clever dick trying to make a point. I thought, time for a word! As I approached the driver's side of the E Type, I could see that the driver was all long blonde hair and large sunglasses and he had a big smile on his face. Before I could say anything, a hand came out of the driver's window to shake mine and he said, "Great job, well done! Keep up the good work." There was Jimmy Savile shaking my hand profusely. We had a quick chat and then back to the point duty. This was of course before the news of all the dreadful allegations made against him in later years.

One of the main celebrity sporting events of the year is the Royal Ascot horse racing meeting held in June every year. It is a wonderful opportunity for all to enjoy and I was very fortunate to have attended on fifteen occasions, mostly with Support Group performing a specialist role. My first time was in 1976. Our initial task was to 'sweep' the route of the Royal procession prior to the Royal party setting off and then provide extra protection until the Queen and her guests were safely in the Royal Enclosure. Once the Royal party was ensconced in their safe surroundings, we had a fairly free role to do foot patrol and assist where required. That first year we were allocated the Grandstand area, doing high profile patrol in an effort to inhibit pickpockets. I soon discovered that the Grandstand area was where the private boxes were located.

One of the features of Royal Ascot is that large crowds; 80,000 on Thursday, Ladies Day, attend to have a good time and for some, that involves a lot of alcohol. Some guests in the private boxes like to invite the patrolling police officers in and even offer them a drink. It is all very pleasant, but it is really hard not to accept while on duty. In the unlikely event of accepting a very weak gin and tonic or the odd glass of champagne care must be taken not to drink too much. I am glad that I was so strong willed.

In the first year, my crewmate and I were invited into a private box in which the American Ambassador and family were guests.

The whole event was a very enjoyable experience. It made a welcome change from some of the more unpleasant tasks we undertook during the rest of the year.

One of the most pleasing encounters I had was meeting the actress Susan George, my second favourite woman in the whole world after my wife of course. She signed her autograph for me with a lovely message, 'For Merv. Lots of love Susan George xxx'.

In 1981 there was great excitement at Ascot when we all saw for the first time the newly engaged Lady Diana Spencer, soon to become Princess Diana. Many millions of words have been written about her. In the ensuing years we were to be involved with Princess Diana's security. It was a privilege to see her close up and witness her ability to engage with people from all walks of life, especially children. She appeared totally at ease in her role and had a knack of making everyone feel special, never failing to acknowledge us with a smile when we were providing protection for her. I will always remember her on that summer's day at Royal Ascot when she looked absolutely stunning.

One of the most charming and friendly people I ever met was also at Royal Ascot, the American actor Douglas Fairbanks Junior. I was in uniform walking from the enclosure towards the main entrance. The walk through the crowded underpass takes quite some time to get through the throng. I found myself next to him as we walked in the same direction. He commented to me about the crush of people and we continued talking about all sorts of things for the duration of our time together. I found it fascinating to listen to him and he was interested in the role of the police at the racecourse. As we parted he shook my hand and thanked me for my company during the previous ten minutes or so. I found him to be courteous and delightful, a true gentleman.

Prince Andrew married Sarah Ferguson in July 1986 and just before the marriage, a major social event to celebrate was held as a private function in Windsor Great Park. Many members of the Royal Family and other high profile guests were attending and the national press were desperate to obtain photographs. In an effort to prevent that occurring and to maintain the necessary security, a major operation was planned. To that end there was an inner cordon and an outer cordon of security. The whole of Support Group were engaged on the event fulfilling various roles.

At one point during the evening, two groups of us met up outside one of the huge marquees where a disco was going full belt. We were checking on our areas of responsibility when we were approached by two of the guests, Billy Connolly and Pamela Stephenson. They enquired if we were okay and was there anything they could do for us, very thoughtful of them. Billy suggested that there was plenty of room on the dance floor in the marquee if we fancied strutting our stuff. We politely declined that one. Nice people taking time to come and say hello was much appreciated. All involved, and the party goers enjoyed themselves in the relaxed and convivial atmosphere long into the night.

I served twice at Gerrards Cross, firstly as a patrol sergeant then later as the inspector in charge of the station. Gerrards Cross and its immediate area is a prime place for celebrity spotting. A great number of them live there.

One afternoon I attended a burglar alarm sounding in an area known to suffer a high level of burglaries. I quickly realised that the owners were not at home, but a first-floor bedroom window had been left open and the wind had probably set the alarm off. A neighbour confirmed everything and produced keys so that we could check the house. He was very helpful and once I had established that everything was in order I was invited to his house for a cup of tea. It was a great pleasure to take tea with Val Doonican in his lounge. I was intrigued to see the famous Red Book on display; he had recently been the subject of 'This Is Your Life'. It was a great honour to look through his Red Book while enjoying tea and biscuits in his company.

Well known local residents in Denham were the acting dynasty of Sir John and Lady Mills, John and Mary Hayley Bell Mills. The first time I attended their home was when the burglar alarm was set off late at night, just after midnight. It appeared that the family were indoors so I went to the front door whilst my colleague checked round the outside of the building. I was met by John Mills who apologised profusely saying that he and his wife, Mary, had just arrived home when she had inadvertently set the alarm off. My colleague confirmed that the outside of the house showed no apparent damage or signs of any break in, but Sir John would not let us leave without us coming in for a cup of tea. It was near Christmas and I was fascinated by the cards on display, one from the Queen Mother being in pride of place. The item which really caught my eye was Sir John's Oscar. When he came in with the tea I remarked about the Oscar which he had been awarded some years earlier for his starring role in the film 'Ryan's Daughter'. He handed it to me and told the story of how heavy it was. He was right, it certainly was. When it was presented to him at the awards ceremony he had to stand and hold it for about forty five minutes and it almost weighed him down. Another memorable event, holding John Mill's Oscar. A really lovely man.

Cilla Black and her husband Bobby lived in the same area in a wonderful big house standing in its own grounds. One summer night I was out on patrol, it was about 2.00am and it appeared quiet everywhere. A friend and colleague of mine, a police dog handler also working nights, called me on the radio and asked to meet up. We were standing talking in a quiet country lane in an area of predominantly large detached houses. We saw an old, quite tatty car being driven slowly up the road towards us. We watched as the car got closer and could see the driver was a young lad looking at the houses as he drove along. We stopped the car (well you would have to wouldn't you?) and asked him the usual, who, what, where and why, questions. To be fair to him, he did have an unusual answer. He said that he was doing a favour for a mate of his, a taxi driver who had taken the night off, so he was taking his mate's place. Apparently, he was looking for Frankie Howerd who was supposed to be at Cilla Black's house waiting for the taxi.

As Cilla's place was very close by and the tale was fairly plausible, I went to her house to ascertain whether his account was true, while my colleague checked out the driver and his story. As I walked down Cilla's gravel drive, beautiful in the moonlight but very noisy to walk on at almost 2.30am, I thought that this could go very wrong if his story didn't check out.

Approaching the house, I heard voices and laughter and could see a light shining out from open patio doors. I went to the door, knocked and saw Cilla Black, her husband Bobby and Frankie Howerd. I apologised for disturbing them and was invited inside; I told them the reason for my being there. Frankie Howerd was not impressed as he had apparently been waiting for his taxi for over an hour. At that point I heard footsteps and looking out, I saw my colleague coming down the gravel drive. He beckoned me out, asking to speak and told me the result of his checks. He then left to return to his dog van where he had left his dog, Sultan, a long haired German shepherd who looked like a bear, to look after the taxi driver!

I found the next bit of the story really funny. I was quite prepared to let Frankie Howerd use it in his act if he wished, but soon realised that it was unlikely to happen. Returning to the house I said, "I have some good news and some bad news. The good news is I can confirm that your taxi has arrived and it is right outside."

Frankie Howerd seemed pleased and said something like, "About time, I've been waiting long enough, but it's here now anyway."

I continued, "But the bad news is, we have just arrested the driver, he is wanted on Warrant in London for non-appearance at court."

Well, Frankie Howerd exploded. Definitely not a happy man. Bobby thought it was enormously funny and I must admit I was with him on that. I attempted to placate the now extremely upset comedian and said that I would take him to the police station at Gerrards Cross where we would contact a local taxi company, who always turned out for us and they would take him home.

So that was it, his Grumpiness came with me and the taxi driver, now a prisoner, went with Dick the dog handler, back to the station to await collection by the Metropolitan Police. My dealings with Cilla and her husband Bobby on that night could not have been any better. They were both charming and most helpful. I wish I could say the same about their guest.

Roy Castle was another local resident in Gerrards Cross, whose house I attended in answer to a burglar alarm. He was most apologetic for me having to attend what turned out to be a false alarm. In keeping with the vast majority of celebrities I have met, he was an absolute delight. He came across exactly the same as his public persona, a genuinely warm, friendly, nice man. It is worth remembering that these celebrities have nothing to prove to me. They are in their own homes, in their own space and so maybe I see 'the real person'. That has been my experience most of the time anyway.

During my second spell at Gerrards Cross, then as an inspector, I was asked to attend a house in Denham to speak to the owners about a wedding they were planning. The house, once lived in by the actor Roger Moore, was now owned by the magician Paul Daniels. The imminent wedding was between him and his assistant the 'lovely' Debbie McGee. I parked in the drive of the beautiful property and was met by Debbie, who really was lovely. She invited me in for coffee and to talk through with Paul the security issues of the property being left unoccupied, whilst the much-publicised wedding was taking place.

They were the perfect hosts and after we had finished the business side of the visit, Paul showed me round the house. This included his collection of magic memorabilia, of which he was justifiably proud. One special item he thought I might have been interested in, was the handcuffs owned by and used in his act by the great magician and escapologist Harry Houdini. He was quite correct, but the word 'interested' does not even half cover it. The handcuffs were a genuine pair of the old barrel type; Paul invited me to put them on and attempt to release them. He placed them on my wrist and try as I might I could not see any way to get them off without the key. He then showed me the trick and how simple and easy it was for Houdini to get out of the handcuffs when he was placed in various seemingly impossible situations. And here was I wearing Houdini's handcuffs, amazing, thank you Paul, a great experience.

NEAR MISSES

One of life's regrets is that I never saw The Beatles perform, my wife did and I am eternally jealous of that. Unfortunately, I never had dealings with any of them either, but I almost met George Harrison. I had an enquiry to carry out regarding an operation at Henley on Thames, which necessitated my calling at George Harrison's wonderful mansion house, Friar Park. The security was as tight as you would expect. I was eventually let into the grounds and made my way to the premises to be met by Peter Harrison, George's brother, out and about in the gardens. George was not at home and although it was tempting to say that I absolutely needed to speak to George himself, that was not true and I was able to resolve my enquiry with Peter. Shame really, but that was as close as I got. What a magnificent house and grounds though and it was a pleasure to see them at close hand.

In a similar vein but under vastly different circumstances, I nearly met a famous rock band and their lead singer, who for now shall remain nameless. Whilst serving with Support Group, one of our annual commitments was to carry out public order and drug patrols at the Reading Rock Festivals.

One year while performing a troubleshooting role with the Support Group, by now as a sergeant on the unit, I was asked to contact the Police Festival Control to be given a sensitive task. I was informed that the Metropolitan Police had been in touch to say that they had a Warrant for the arrest of the lead singer, which they had been unable to execute for some time. They were aware that he was with his band who were performing that afternoon at Reading Rock. I was asked to execute the Warrant and arrest him. I made some enquiries on the site and was told that as soon as the group had finished their set they were being whisked away. To that end I formed a plan and briefed my officers. We would wait out of sight in the wings and as soon as the group had taken their places in front of the audience we would enter stage left and 'swift' the lead singer away. My team loved the idea and the proposal.

As a matter of courtesy, I spoke with the superintendent in overall charge of the event and shared my plan with him. To say that he was not impressed was a bit of an understatement. There was no way he was going to let us anywhere near the stage and an arrest was totally out of the question. He was really concerned that we would be responsible for starting a riot. Well that was nothing new, we were always being accused of doing that, but this time I could see his point of view and he was probably right. The upshot was that the group did their full set on stage and were 'swifted' away before anyone could get anywhere near them. We were not allowed to even try to arrest him. Shame really, it would have been interesting to say the least.

Although this does not qualify for a 'celebrity I have met' entry, it was one of the most unforgettable events of all the Reading Rock Festivals I attended. Over the years I have seen some top bands performing at the festival. The highlight was on the last night of the Reading Festival in 1992. After I had finished my duty for the day, I met my two sons, Gareth and Matthew, then aged 17 and 14 years. I had managed to obtain tickets to see the headline band for the closing night, Nirvana, with lead singer Kurt Cobain. There we were in wellies, wrapped up warm standing outside in the mud, very near the front of the stage watching Nirvana perform their set, including their big hit Smells Like Teen Spirit; it was amazing. This is often regarded as one of the most iconic festival moments and one of their most memorable performances and we were there, sadly never to be seen again after Kurt Cobain committed suicide. It was for us, just fantastic. We have been to many gigs of all sorts both before and since but that takes some beating. In fact it was so memorable that the band's name is made reference to in the title of this book.

Much later in my service when I was superintendent in charge of Operational Support, I was invited to give a presentation at a conference. The subject was Planning for Terrorism – Chemical, Biological, Radiological and Nuclear (CBRN). The good news was that the conference was in Las Vegas, USA. On about my third conference, again held in Las Vegas, I was staying in the hotel Harrahs on The Strip, where the event took place. By now I had got to know a few of the other presenters, all from the USA; Police, Fire, Ambulance or FBI. One of them pointed me in the direction of another conference taking place in the same hotel. This was a firearms dealer's conference, a Gun Show, where guns were openly displayed and for sale. I took a look and found it mind blowing. It took place in a room the size of a large hanger, set out like a giant market with rows and rows of stalls all full of guns of all descriptions and associated equipment. Without doubt the most interesting stall holder and firearms dealer I met, was Tom Selleck. Probably best known as the actor who played the part of Magnum PI and the New York Police Commissioner, Frank Reagan, in the TV series Blue Bloods. I didn't realise until then that Tom was a very keen firearms dealer in his own right, as well as being a top notch actor. His business partner on the stall tried to sell a gun and holster to me, but I had to explain that there was no way that could happen. Imagine the problems trying to bring that through the 'Anything to Declare' channel back at Heathrow?

CHAPTER 7

—

Where Duty Calls

Rabbit again!

The Queen was visiting the new city of Milton Keynes in June 1979 and Support Group was assisting local officers by supplementing their numbers with a uniformed presence. We were all there bright and early, best uniform, out and about in the city making sure everything was in order. As the Queen and Prince Philip started a walkabout, we were asked to fill in the police lines in the shopping area to give a greater police representation. There was I in the line of local police officers with the walkabout in full swing, when Prince Philip reached me, he stopped and asked me. "How long have you been stationed at Milton Keynes?" I explained that extra police had been drafted in for the day and that I was one of them. A couple of easier questions and it was all over and he moved on.

Some time later while working in the Oxford area, we were aware that trouble had been brewing on the Blackbird Leys housing estate in Cowley. It came to a head one evening when local police officers attempting to make an arrest of a local youth, were attacked by a large crowd and had to withdraw. The officers called for assistance and we responded, that was part of our role to assist local officers in difficult circumstances. It was obvious immediately that this was the spark which ignited something out of the ordinary. During the night petrol bombs were thrown at police and at local buildings. We were fully kitted up in riot gear and eventually cleared the streets. The following evening with what appeared to be the world's press gathered, it all kicked off again with a young woman and her boyfriend being attacked by local youths and suffering serious injuries. The petrol bombing started again and that was the formula for several nights; petrol bombs, police in riot gear and at the appropriate time and location, clearing the streets and making arrests. After several nights of this and significant arrests it quietened down and the area slowly returned to normality.

April 1980 – I was called out from my home address in the early hours of the morning to a firearms incident at Woodley, near Reading. A short time before there had been a shooting in London outside the Regents Park mosque when a Libyan journalist, who had been campaigning against the Libyan leader Colonel Gaddafi, had been shot dead. Two men, believed to be Libyan students, were arrested nearby after they fired shots at police and other people from the mosque. Intelligence was to hand that a male person connected with the shooting was at a house in Woodley. We armed up nearby, put an armed containment on the house and prepared to crash the front door and arrest the person in the house. With others, I was on outside containment at the front of the house covering the front door once the raid team had entered. It took several attempts to crash the door with a sledgehammer, but eventually it gave way and the team was in.

At that point I heard glass smashing above me and a man of Eastern European appearance landed on the lawn close to me. He had jumped through the first floor bedroom window, smashing it as he did so. I stood over him and confronted him at gunpoint, was joined by my crewmate and we secured him. He had a badly gashed leg where he had jumped straight through the glass. The situation was contained and the ambulance crew we had standing by were called in to treat his injuries before he was taken to hospital. Together with my crewmate we accompanied him in the ambulance.

On arrival we were met by a rather severe looking Nursing Sister, who was not happy about having two heavy looking armed officers in her hospital. Once we had explained what had led up to us being there and that we were required to stay close to the injured man, she was wonderful. She was however, clearly unimpressed with our prisoner. I must have missed it when they gave him the anaesthetic, either that or it wasn't very effective because it didn't half hurt when they stitched him up.

All the nursing staff were brilliant. It transpired that our prisoner was the suspect we were looking for. At our de-brief it was revealed that as the raid team were running up the stairs of the house, he jumped from his bed straight through the bedroom window. He was a Libyan student living in the rented accommodation with his wife and family. His version of events was that he was woken by the front door being crashed in and thought it was criminals getting into his house. Looking out of his bedroom window he saw many policemen outside and thinking they were chasing the criminals he threw himself to the police by smashing and jumping through the first floor window! Once he had been released from hospital he was handed over to CID and Special Branch officers, who could start their investigation.

MAJOR EXERCISES

Every year one police force is allocated a major exercise by the Home Office; this is a very important major event. It is at least twelve months in the planning stage and is a multi agency exercise eventually involving a vast number of personnel. We were aware that TVP had been selected this year to host the exercise to take place in May 1980. It would relate to a terrorist incident to which we would initially respond as a police firearms team and then ultimately, Special Forces would take over towards the end of the exercise and resolve it. We were not aware of any other details. What we could not have known was that later, events in London would change everything.

On 30th April 1980, seven heavily armed Iranian separatist gunmen entered the Iranian Embassy in Prince's Gate, London taking embassy staff, a policeman and a number of visitors hostage. During the course of the next six days, the siege attracted unprecedented global media attention. On Saturday 5th May a member of the embassy staff was shot and killed by the terrorists and then thrown out of the front door. A unit from the Special Air Service (SAS) implemented their plan and attacked the building by multiple entries. The result was that they killed all but one of the terrorists and saved nineteen hostages, including the police officer. All this took place under the glare and spotlight of the world's media. It was a landmark in counter terrorism operations.

Fairly soon after the siege had been resolved, we were informed that our major exercise was to be postponed. What we did not realise until then, was that the SAS team taking part in our exercise was the same team who stormed the Iranian Embassy and they had some issues to address. One of the troopers had got stuck whilst abseiling from the roof and when stun grenades had been thrown into one of the rooms, the curtains caught fire which should not have happened.

After a few weeks our exercise took place in the wilds of the Berkshire Downs. Before it commenced we met with the SAS team who had arrived to prepare for their involvement. It was great to have the opportunity to meet them and have a coffee and a chat before it all got going. They were first rate people, very ordinary and unspectacular until the real business started when they took over from us.

Once everything was underway we deployed at various points surrounding a house where the 'terrorists' had barricaded themselves in with 'hostages'. Presently, the time came for us to be relieved by our military colleagues. One of our team had taken up a good vantage point a few feet off the ground up a tree. He was told over the radio that his military relief was on his way and would be with him in ten minutes. After that amount of time he said out loud to no-one in particular, "Well where is he then?" A reply came from somewhere below him, "I'm here, you can come down now."

When 'one of our finest' looked down to see who was speaking to him he couldn't see anyone. Eventually a 'bush' pulled his trouser leg and said, "Here I am." Sure enough, there he was, completely disguised. Brilliant!

A number of us were very fortunate to see some of their action and it was an absolute privilege to see them operate.

In November 1980 I was called to a briefing with the whole of Support Group. There, we were informed that we would be engaged full time over the next few weeks on armed guard duties. Our task was to protect another 'Supergrass' who would this time be appearing at Oxford Crown Court to give evidence. As mentioned earlier, we had been involved once before in 1977 in a similar protection operation. The supergrass this time was a man named Roger Dennhardt, he gave his occupation as Armed Robber. He had been the leader of a gang who had committed a number of armed robberies; in one incident a security guard had been shot. When he and the gang were captured, he was looking at a substantial term of imprisonment. He offered to turn Queens Evidence and 'grass' on other members of his gang, thus clearing up a whole host of serious crimes.

Our job was to protect him round the clock, get him to and from the Crown Court and ensure that the whole building and environs were secure. We were also responsible for searching everyone entering the court complex. Armed officers were stationed in and around the court as well as in the actual courtroom whilst Dennhardt was giving evidence. I met him immediately before his first appearance. I was struck by what a charismatic person he appeared to be. He was very smartly dressed, expensive suit, hair just right, very polite, a charming man. He told me that he had spent the previous evening going over his statement because he wanted to make sure everything went well. It ran to more than 900 pages, and attention to detail was very important to him.

The whole operation was an interesting one. The staff working in the court complex were understanding and very quickly became used to our searching methods and questions. Not so, some of the many lawyers. There were six other defendants charged with numerous serious offences and each one had their own legal team. One barrister in particular, he was a defence QC, was especially difficult and every day he complained incessantly about himself and his bags being searched and how pointless it was.

During the second day of the operation a female member of the court staff passed a clever remark. This was the first time I had heard it, although I did hear it several times in later years but the first time is always the best, so they say. I was stationed in a corridor immediately behind the judge's door leading into court, providing armed security and a sterile area for the judge. For appearance sake, we were dressed in normal uniform. I had my revolver in a holster under the tunic making it stand out quite a lot. The attractive young lady whom we had spoken to a few times, came along the corridor with a message to leave for the judge. She explained where she needed to go and then said to me, "Are you carrying a gun or are you just pleased to see me?" Corny I know, but it made my day.

About one week into the operation I was doing a tour of duty inside the courtroom, sitting at the back so that all the court and people present were within my view. The supergrass had been in the witness box all day giving evidence and was now being cross examined, by the grumpy barrister who complained every morning when we searched him. The barrister was concentrating on a particular line of questioning. I eventually saw where he was leading. He spent about an hour asking questions about an armed robbery committed by the gang some years before in Bedfordshire. What he was leading up to in a measured, laborious way was the fact that the supergrass had committed the armed robbery. Then later at the Crown Court, he had vehemently denied it on oath. The point being made was that if he had lied on oath previously, why should he be believed on oath now. An excellent and pertinent point. When the barrister had laid out all the groundwork for the jury to see where he was going with his questions, he socked it to the supergrass by saying, "Isn't it a fact that you lied on oath at the Crown Court about committing that armed robbery?"

Without hesitation the supergrass replied, "Well you should know, you were my barrister and you were representing me." He told us afterwards that was true. The court was in uproar, the jury was laughing, court officials were trying not to laugh, the judge attempted to restore some order and the line of questioning the barrister had been working on for over an hour, had been destroyed.

The end result was that the majority of the defendants were convicted and the three main offenders were sentenced to a total of one hundred and eighty two years. The supergrass was sentenced to eight years imprisonment. Normally he would have expected three times that sentence and he had already served a substantial amount of his term in custody whilst being protected.

The story does not end there. After a relatively short time in prison, he was released. I mentioned previously that he was a charismatic person; obviously I was not alone in thinking this. He had clearly made an impression on a Detective Sergeant who had been his minder during a lot of time in police custody. When he was released from prison he teamed up with the sergeant and together they committed a robbery on a security van delivering to a Post Office. They got away with a substantial amount of money. It wasn't long before the police officer was caught, stood trial and was sentenced to nine years imprisonment. By then Dennhardt had disappeared and was out of the country.

THE BBC POLICE PROGRAMME

In January 1982, BBC television started showing a new series called 'Police' which was filmed solely within the TVP area. For some months the makers of the programme had been given unprecedented access to film with patrolling officers and behind the scenes within the police stations. This was one of the earliest reality TV shows; it was well publicised and eagerly awaited. Probably the most controversial episode, featured an interview by CID officers at Reading Police Station. They were interviewing a possible rape victim and there was controversy about the manner in which she was treated. The impression given on camera was that they did not believe her and consequently gave her a hard time over her allegation. It was so controversial that it changed the way rape allegations were dealt with from thereon.

I featured in a couple of episodes and one in particular was memorable.

In August of the previous year I was still on Support Group and we were working at the annual Reading Rock Festival engaged on crime and drug patrols. During the Saturday afternoon, a motorist reported that on returning to his car parked in a side street near the festival site he found the street full of drunken festival goers, some of whom were dancing on the roof of his car. My crewmate Tony and I were nearby, and we took the call to attend. As we turned into the road we were confronted by the street packed with what appeared to be festival goers having a street party and totally blocking the road.

I saw a lady about halfway along the street trying to get into her car, a new Volvo, she looked very upset. There were two people dancing on the roof of her car. Tony and I approached the car and one of the youths saw us, jumped off and disappeared into the crowd. The other one with his back to us, was still jumping up and down on the roof when I grabbed him and hauled him off. I could see that the roof had several dents in it so shouted in his ear, because the noise of the crowd was deafening, that he was under arrest for criminal damage. I put him in the back seat of our unmarked police vehicle.

At that point the crowd surrounded our car and started chanting for him to be released. We had already called for more officers as soon as we turned into the road, but now we put in a call for assistance. Some of the crowd were pushing against the car and trying to open the door to get my prisoner out. I stood on one side, by the door, and Tony stood the other. People were shouting, "You are not going to take him. We will get him out." They were making all sorts of threats. Tony and I were telling them that if they moved back away from the vehicle, we would listen to them. We were playing for time, thinking that any second now the troops would arrive, and we would be okay. At that point 'assistance' did arrive in the form of the local bobby for that area, the community beat officer with his pushbike. He came from the opposite end of the street pushing his bike through the crowd saying, "Make way, make way, let me through, what's going on?"

He made it as far as our car and his contribution was, "Well they (the crowd) are only here because you are here. If you leave they will go." Fat chance of that with the crowd totally surrounding our car! And with that he was off, pushing his bike through the throng back the way he had come. Well thanks for your help! It did take the sting out of the situation for a few moments, some of the crowd found it funny. We made another call for assistance because we were still alone with the prisoner and the crowd. I could not understand why the rest of our lot had not yet turned up to help.

Normally in a situation like this, the rest of the Support Group would be with us within seconds, but it felt like we were waiting for an extremely long time. In fact, it turned out to be less than ten minutes. The next 'assistance' to arrive was the BBC TV film crew filming for the Police series. We already knew them because they had been on other operations with us. They pushed their way through and continued filming. Again, this took the sting out of things with a lot of the crowd thinking that it was a TV news film crew and they would be on the telly. There was still no police back-up in sight, so we put in a further call for much needed help. At last the cavalry arrived in the form of other Support Group officers. Our colleagues piled out, got a quick brief from us and started pushing the crowd back away from our car.

Within a couple of minutes, we were able to reverse the car out and take our prisoner to the police station. With him safely booked in, a quick visit to the control room was in order. Why, with over one hundred officers close by when we were calling for assistance, had it taken close on ten minutes for us to get help? The answer was simple. When we first asked for help, in the next street Drug Squad officers were trying to make an arrest and called for assistance. Within seconds back up for them arrived, their situation was resolved so the message then went out cancelling all assistance and everyone took this to mean at our location. The second time we called for assistance again the message was broadcast, "No, cancel. That has already been sorted out." It wasn't until our third call that the penny dropped, and help was sent to us. It was a difficult situation which almost got out of hand. It was a bit hairy for a little while, but such is life.

In July 1981, the inevitable happened. Eventually, everyone must leave Support Group and go back to normal policing, whatever normal is. Without exception we were all reluctant to do so. Sometimes the one leaving had to practically have their fingers prised off the steering wheel of the car. It softens the blow if they can go on to something which they really want to do, that was the case for me. I had managed to eke out close to six years on the group and my last day was a Saturday, the final day at Royal Ascot, a sad day for me. At the hot debrief at Ascot under the trees with all the Support Group officers present, Ted Molyneux our Chief Inspector, the boss, said that as well as it being the end of Royal Ascot week it was also farewell to Smurf, his nickname for me.

With best wishes from all there, I was gone, cast out and onto pastures new. As of the following Monday, I started a new exciting phase of my career as a patrol sergeant at Gerrards Cross.

CHAPTER 8

—

The Thin Blue Line

The thin blue line

I t was a bit of a culture shock in the beginning. Having worked for nearly six years with very experienced, skilled officers, I was now a patrol sergeant with few resources and some, bright new youngsters, looking for guidance as they embarked on their police careers. One of the advantages of being a sergeant is that you choose, where and with whom to go out on patrol. Early on at a new station especially on promotion, it is like starting all over again and I preferred to go out on my own to get to know my patch. With daytime shifts, I would go out on foot patrol to meet the local people and support the Bobbies on their beat. It was suggested by older and wiser colleagues that, as a newly promoted sergeant, when I did so it was worth visiting the High Street. The reason for this was that you could admire yourself in the large plate glass windows, to see what you looked like with your three new shiny, white stripes. There were a number of such shop windows in Gerrards Cross High Street, so I am told!

I was shown the ropes by an experienced sergeant, which was a great help. He presented me with an 'in' tray containing reports and files for prosecution from my shift of officers. As the sergeant, I had to make recommendations on whether to prosecute or not. Previously as a constable, I was used to submitting my files to the sergeant for those recommendations or the report was sent back for more evidence or further enquiries. Now I was that sergeant and the initial decision was mine. Frightening. Apart from advice from the other sergeants, there was very little help in those days to assist in making such decisions. There was a Newly Promoted Sergeants Course, quite good, but not much help when you attended it nine months after being promoted!

It was a steep learning curve, but I enjoyed the responsibility, especially having two young probationers (new police officers within their first two years of service). I hoped that I could help them with my experience of now nearly ten years service. One of the difficulties I faced was the shortage of officers. When we paraded for my first week of nights, 2200 – 0600 hours, there were four of us, including me plus one for the front desk. The police station was open twenty-four hours a day.

I remained in this role for eighteen months and loved it, although I did miss the life I had grown used to as a Support Group officer. There were some memorable events during my time at Gerrards Cross.

Early into my tenure as a new patrol sergeant I was on early turn, 0600 – 1400 hours, when at about 0800 hours one morning I was contacted by the duty inspector, who always prosecuted at the weekly Wednesday Beaconsfield Magistrates Court. Unfortunately, he could not take the court that day, therefore the early turn sergeant always prosecuted in his place. "Yes, that seems okay, thanks for letting me know."

Hang on, I thought, that's me! WHAT? Me, prosecuting and in two hours time? That is not possible. I don't know what to do or how to do it. These and other negative thoughts sped through my mind. Panic set in. "No problem," he said. "The Clerk of the Court is aware, he will see you through it. The papers are at court awaiting your arrival, just have a look through, stand up, address the magistrates and read out the statement of facts."

That didn't sound too bad. Only motoring stuff, a bit of illegal parking and so on. "No 'not guilty' pleas then?" I said stupidly.

"Oh yes," he replied. "But straightforward; 'driving without due care and attention' and one other. It's all in the papers, you will be fine. Just speak to Richard, the Clerk." And he was gone!

Well, where was the training? I never signed up for this! I had no desire to be a Perry Mason striding about the court with thumbs hooked under my armpits, which was the image going through my mind. No choice, so off I went, smart new tunic with the brand spanking new, bright white stripes shining out like a beacon. On reaching the court at Beaconsfield, I was handed all the files to be prosecuted BY ME! More shocks. There were loads of files and I had to read through them and try to remember the order of events from when I had previously given evidence in court. On those previous appearances all I was required to do was give evidence but not today, there was much more to it.

I sifted through the files making notes at the side of the papers. I had seen that done on television and it seemed the right the thing to do. I hoped it looked like I knew what I was doing. HA!

I arrived early and had the courtroom to myself. All too soon, Richard came in and introduced himself. What a really nice man, young like me, very friendly and so helpful. I managed a few words and he soon realised that I was a virgin prosecutor. He assured me that it would be no problem; he had seen it all before and done this lots of times with 'newbies'. "It will be fine," he said. "Oh, and one other thing, the magistrates will want to see you in their room. Nothing to worry about, they like to see the new sergeants when they first start. They will just ask you about the cases which are up today." WHAT? Discussing the cases with the magistrates before it all starts, oh no! I thought strongly for a moment about making a run for it, turning in my stripes and seeing if they would have me back on Support Group.

Before I knew it, Richard was back in court saying, "The magistrates would like to see you before we start." I was ushered into their room and introduced. They all seemed very nice. The chairman of the bench asked, "What have we got up before us today? Nothing too bad I see. Is there anything we should know or any problems you can foresee?" How the hell should I know, I hadn't got a clue? Fortunately, I didn't say that, I think I mumbled something about it all looking okay and straightforward. We were just about to find out.

Within a few minutes I was in position in front of the magistrates, the Clerk, the people in the public seats and the local press. Away we went. It was all a bit of a blur really. I remember standing up at the right times, mostly, reading out what I was supposed to and then the defendant was called for the not guilty driving offence. Worse was to come, he was represented by a solicitor who came into court and sat alongside, a few yards away from me. He nodded a sort of greeting. I think I just glared at him, he was the opposition after all and we were just about to do battle. Then the case started and surprisingly it wasn't too bad. It was a bit like interviewing a suspect out on the street or at the police station, something I was comfortable with. I cross- examined the defendant and he seemed more nervous than me as I started to warm to the task. I picked up on a couple of things he had said, which I thought weakened his story and then it was over.

The magistrates retired to consider their verdict; I was told later that it was time for their coffee and biscuits, but that is very unfair. Maybe they needed time to digest the magnificent performance of the new prosecutor and the high level of evidence he had produced! Whilst they were out, there was a three-way general conversation between the solicitor, the Clerk and me. We spoke about legal and lawyerly things, I almost sounded like I knew what I was talking about. After twenty minutes the magistrates returned and found the defendant guilty. GUILTY! I had won my first case as a prosecutor. I could get used to this, maybe even take up being a barrister. Hold on, slow down, let's not get carried away.

Before much longer it was all over, and the cases were finished. I thanked Richard profusely; he was a calming influence and helped me through proceedings. He said that it was fine with no problems and I had done well. Maybe he was just being kind. Everyone to their own, but in truth, that prosecuting lark was not for me. I was grateful that was my one and only time. I would rather face armed criminals any day, at least I knew what I was doing.

A couple of months after my promotion we were on nights. It was fairly busy for a normally quiet patch, covering Gerrards Cross, Denham, the Chalfonts and Beaconsfield. Sometime after midnight, we had a radio message to say that a man had been seen breaking into a garage at Chalfont St Peter. The double crewed car for that area was despatched and I would back them up patrolling in the transit van. The car was crewed by Phil, who was my lieutenant, a PC with about the same service as me. He was very good and knew the area better than anyone. He had with him a young probationer, Grant, we were both trying to encourage him to be a little more assertive. He was a big lad but was a mite timid and needed to push himself. He had only been in the job a few months and not being local he didn't know the area at all.

I found the other two already at the scene, there were signs of a break in. Phil suggested where we should look and that if we split up, we could cover all the likely places where the offender might be. This we did. After about ten minutes I heard Grant calling, "I've got him!" Followed by lots of shouting. Phil and I ran towards where the noise was coming from. As I arrived the offender had just broken free after apparently thumping Grant. We managed to get hold of him and detained and handcuffed him. Grant had done a really good job and we had the offender in custody.

Phil informed me that he was a well-known local villain with lots of previous convictions. He was a big lad and had some previous (a police term meaning that a suspect has previous convictions) for assault on police as well as a string of other offences. What upset me most was that he had had a real go at Grant. This young officer was just starting out on his police career and this bastard had given him a hard time. Grant was in my charge and I was annoyed that this local toe-rag had treated him so roughly. I ensured that he was handcuffed correctly and we put him in the back of the transit van with some difficulty as he was not being very co-operative and was struggling.

Grant came back with me in the van to the police station at Tatling End, so that I could check that he was alright after his altercation. We met Phil back at the station. All the way there, our man in the back was making threats about what he was going to do to Grant and me once we stopped. He was a real 'hard man' and he was intent on showing us just how hard he was. Back at the police station, the rear door had been opened for us and I reversed right up to it. Matey was used to being arrested and being fairly well treated by the local police. I had been dealing with people like him for the past six years, although he and I had never met before tonight. When I opened the van door I asked the prisoner to get out. He replied by telling me what he was going to do to me and all the police in Gerrards Cross. Apparently, something very unpleasant, interspersed with threats and obscenities. He also said, "If you want me out, come and get me."

He was clearly refusing to get out of the van and despite me asking him nicely on several occasions he still refused and continued to make threats. As we had not met before I introduced myself to him and told him his future. Under such circumstances where someone continues to be unco-operative you have to grab the initiative so he was eventually forcibly removed from the back of the transit van and put in the detention room. I removed the handcuffs and he immediately adopted a hostile stance. I persuaded him that it was not a good idea to be so aggressive. He quietened down a little and mentioned that he had never seen me before. According to him I was the aggressive one because he had been hurt when he was removed from the van. It is inevitable when someone is fighting and struggling and refusing to co-operate that they may be hurt and I pointed this out to him. I told him that I was okay with him having a go at me, but I was upset that he had given Grant a hard time. He apologised and said that he was only trying to get away and would like to apologise to the young PC if he was allowed to. This took place later. When I left him, we were almost the best of friends! Well we must have been, he pleaded guilty to all charges and made no complaints.

One Saturday evening we reported for night duty at 9.45pm and were immediately turned out to assist colleagues at High Wycombe, where problems in the town centre were escalating. That turned out to be an understatement. During the summer there had been outbreaks of public disorder in various parts of the UK and now it had reached High Wycombe.

After a quick briefing at High Wycombe police station we deployed around the town where 100 to 150 youths were clearly intent on causing major trouble. Pretty soon windows were being smashed. When police responded we were faced with a barrage of missiles and then the petrol bombs started. A police transit van with ten officers on board was attacked, windows of the vehicle smashed and a petrol bomb was thrown through the broken window. It hit the shoulder of one officer and petrol spilled all over him. Fortunately, those idiots did not know that they were supposed to light the rag in the petrol bomb before it was thrown. How lucky was that officer? Some police units deployed in protective gear with riot shields, whilst the remainder patrolled in numbers sweeping up around the edges. It took several hours to fully regain control and restore order, the final tally being eleven police officers injured and a number of arrests made. A total of forty shops had suffered smashed windows, damage and looting.

During my patrols I came around the corner at the edge of the town centre shops and I saw a young man on the pavement, in the process of looting a gent's outfitters. When he saw the police car he ran off with a tailor's dummy dressed in a dinner suit complete with dress shirt and bow tie. If he had to stoop to looting, I could almost understand stealing the latest expensive audio equipment or high-end stuff, but a dinner suit and bow tie, come on! He deserved to get caught and he was, after a short chase during which he ditched the dummy. He appeared to be the most unlikely person to need a dinner suit. When I spoke to him he didn't even want one and it wasn't his size anyway.

The following night there were similar problems but scaled down and the police were out on the streets early in greater numbers.

By August 1981, mainly because of my experience with Support Group in dealing with major public disorder, I was able to take one of the sergeant's places on the Police Support Unit (PSU). This is in addition to an officer's normal duty. It is strictly volunteers only who receive regular, specialist training to deal with public disorder. It has changed since, but then a PSU was made up of one inspector, three sergeants and thirty constables. They deployed in three units of ten officers, each with a sergeant in charge and the inspector in overall command. Whenever there was a request for mutual aid assistance from anywhere in our force area or in the UK, PSUs were sent.

One month after the High Wycombe troubles, that is exactly what happened. There had been problems in Liverpool with street disorder and it was escalating to mammoth proportions. Three PSUs were sent from TVP, mine included. We were expected to be away for several days over a long weekend. We travelled to Liverpool by coach and were billeted at the university. We found out on arrival that just about every police force in England and Wales had sent officers to assist in what was expected to be, major public disorder throughout the city.

On the Saturday there was a huge march organised against the Chief Constable, Kenneth Oxford, it was dubbed the Oxford Out March. Liverpool traffic police officers were allocated to us as the drivers of our transit vans. On the way to our duty assembly point, they took us on a tour of Toxteth where some of the worst rioting had taken place. We saw where the famous Rialto Cinema had recently been destroyed by fire and numerous properties gutted or burnt to the ground. We deployed in the city centre ready for the march. Many times, we were approached by local people, who said that they could see by our helmet plates that we were not from Liverpool. They were interested to know where we were from and why we were there. They also said that they were pleased to see us, thanked us for coming all that way and that if we were patrolling in their area we were invited to call in for a cup of tea. They also made it very plain that whilst they would be pleased to see us call in for tea and biscuits, our local police driver was not welcome. They really did not like the 'bizzies', the name they used for local officers.

The first part of the march progressed without incident, but trouble wasn't far away. One police officer was attacked, badly beaten and stabbed in the stomach. Another was stabbed in the shoulder and we were taking many other injuries. We moved to standby at the new police station which was opposite the new Liverpool Cathedral. Reports were coming in that hundreds of youths were besieging the police station in Toxteth. No one could get in or out of the immediate area around the police station. Plans were being formulated for our deployment. We were also informed at the briefing that the greatest of care needed to be taken on deployment. There had been a rash of burglaries at sports shops throughout Liverpool. No one could get hold of a javelin for love nor money, they were all stolen and expected to be in the arsenal of weapons of the youths intent on confrontation. We understood the dangers only too well because we had previously tested them in our PSU training, javelins and crossbow bolts, which had also been stolen in great numbers, go straight through riot shields.

Well, there we were standing by, waiting to be deployed, ready for the worst case scenario, but this is what we were trained for. Then suddenly, we were stood down and told to return to our billets at the university. WHAT? WHY? Here we were in great numbers. There were sixty five PSUs, that is over 2,000 police officers, trained to deal with exactly the problem happening just about ten minutes away. Our Liverpool police colleagues were besieged in their own police station by hundreds of people, as well as rioting in the surrounding streets and we could sort this out. Unfortunately, we did not have the opportunity to do so. We were champing at the bit to assist our colleagues but had no say in the matter. Maybe in slow time, I could have understood the reason for us not getting the go ahead. Without doubt we could have sorted out the problem on that day, but what would the longer-term implications have been for Liverpool and Toxteth in particular and for local police officers? It was however an unforgettable experience and the local Liverpool people we met who made us welcome were brilliant. The reception and greeting from them was heart-warming.

By January 1983, I had spent an enjoyable eighteen months as a patrol sergeant at Gerrards Cross and learnt a great deal, but on being offered the opportunity to return to the job that I really loved, it was no contest. When given the chance to return to Support Group as one of the four sergeants, there wasn't a moment's hesitation. At last, I was back!

CHAPTER 9

—

Support Group Sergeant

"In tow"

Greenham Common – One of my first duties on returning to Support Group was policing a protest at the old RAF airfield at Upper Heyford, Oxfordshire. At this time it was being used as an important strategic US Air Force base. There were a few sporadic protests there mainly against cruise missiles being based in the UK and in that area. However, our main involvement with such cruise missile protests was at Greenham Common, Newbury. The organisation of this major, and what transpired to be long running, protest was well under way. A permanent protest camp was established near the main entrance to the American air base. Other camps grew up at times at different locations around the nine miles of the perimeter fence. The camp at the main entrance was always the focal point and it remained in place for some years, long after the cruise missiles had been removed back to the USA. The unique nature of this protest was that it was strictly women only, 'wimmen' as some of them preferred to be known. They did enforce this rule and in the early days when male protesters arrived for specific days they were quickly and forcibly told to bugger off and protest somewhere else.

The Support Group plus local officers and PSUs for major organised days of protest were regularly employed to police the Greenham Women. The camp was in place close to the main gate for more than five years, before it was eventually removed by bailiffs.

In September 1983, at 2.30am it was one of those now familiar callouts from home to a firearms incident. It was reported as a Hells Angels party at Cookham which had gone badly wrong, two people had been dropped off at separate hospitals, both were dead.

I called my team out and went with Noel, my crewmate for travelling purposes. We went straight to the scene of the party and were briefed by the local police commander. Apparently, a group of about one hundred and fifty Hells Angels had been having a party, which was called to make peace and 'heal old wounds' between The Windsor Chapter and The All England Chapter. Groups of bikers called The Road Rats and Satan's Slaves were also involved. Four years earlier, rival groups of Hells Angels clashed in the New Forest and the Windsor leader was shot and badly wounded. There had been problems since then. The party was at two cottages on open land between Cookham and Maidenhead, Berkshire. The properties were unoccupied and hidden behind a high wall with access straight off the road, through a door in the wall.

There had been complaints of noise during the evening and a local police officer responded. He opened the door giving access to the land and cottages and was confronted by the sight of groups of Hells Angels enjoying themselves and taking part in an axe throwing competition. There was a lot of heavy drinking, dozens of motor bikes everywhere and general uncontrolled mayhem. The officer surveyed the scene for a moment and then with his hand still on the door, shouted, "Keep the noise down will you? I don't want to have to come back and tell you again." He then closed the door behind him, got into the police car and drove away. Good for him, what a very sensible thing to do. He made a full report to the control room and therefore when the bodies turned up at the hospitals, the connection was made and on call out we were directed to the cottages.

Something must have sparked violence. At 1.30am a man was deposited at High Wycombe hospital, he was dead from stab wounds. Thirty minutes later a second group on motor bikes turned up at Wexham Park hospital, Slough with another dead man. His throat had been cut.

While waiting for the rest of the team and our firearms to arrive, Noel and I had a quick, discreet recce. We could see the vast area of open land, a large marquee with enough booze to stock a medium size pub, and the cottages. A lot of Hells Angels were in and around the two dwellings, some lying on the ground. When the team arrived we quickly armed up out in the road, put an armed containment on the cottages and began arresting all those outside. We started calling everyone out of the houses, one at a time, at gunpoint. Each was questioned when they came out as to how many remained inside.

Eventually it appeared that there was only a handful left. When no one else came out voluntarily, we executed an armed raid on the cottages and swept up one of two more. We found one man in an upstairs bedroom who was unconscious with an axe wound in his head. Another one was lying on a bed with a stab wound to his stomach and the whole of the front of his shirt covered in blood. We treated him until it was safe for the ambulance crew to take over. I thought he was dead for sure, but he did recover later in hospital. A search of the cottages revealed an assortment of weapons, some bloodstained. There had been one very clever attempt to conceal a shotgun, but we found it after a thorough search.

We arrested twenty-eight people on suspicion of murder at the cottages that night, out of a total of fifty-one arrests made.

For some days in April 1984, we had all been watching events unfold on national television which reported the tragic murder of WPC Yvonne Fletcher, the Metropolitan police officer shot dead in St James Square, London whilst on duty. On 17th April 1984 an anti-Gaddafi demonstration by Libyan students took place and WPC Fletcher was helping control the small demonstration outside the Libyan People's Bureau, the Libyan Embassy. Without warning and for no apparent reason, automatic gunfire came from within the embassy. Yvonne Fletcher was hit in the stomach and died soon after at Westminster Hospital. Ten other people, students taking part in the demonstration, were injured by the gunfire.

The Metropolitan Police surrounded the embassy and it was the subject of an armed siege for the next eleven days. During that time no one entered or left the building. Eventually it became apparent that the occupants had agreed to leave the building under police escort, on the understanding that they would all be allowed to return to Libya. The evening before this was due to take place I, together with the other Support Group supervisors, were called to TVP HQ and briefed regarding the Libyans being escorted from their embassy. We were informed that we would play a major part in it. Owing to the sensitive nature of the operation, the occupants of the embassy were to be escorted to the Civil Service College at Sunningdale, Berkshire, in our area, hence the reason for our involvement. We were to be armed for the operation.

On the proposed day at 9.50am, the first group of Libyans came out of the embassy and followed instructions to the letter. They walked out in single file, a total of thirty of them. They travelled in a convoy of twenty-eight vehicles and were escorted to Sunningdale. On arrival they were housed in a number of rooms, whilst the 'formalities' were completed by other agencies. I was involved in the security inside the building and came across one of the Libyans when I used the toilet. Whilst standing there I looked across at him and he looked at me. I remember thinking, 'It could have been you. You may be the one who shot Yvonne Fletcher, if not you probably know who did, you bastard.' I must say he looked especially sheepish, but I suppose that is only to be expected under the circumstances. Shortly after that with the formalities apparently completed, they were returned to the vehicles and escorted to Heathrow Airport and away to Libya. No one was identified as the shooter. No police investigation was permitted. No detailed questioning of them was allowed in an attempt to find out who was responsible for shooting our police colleague.

I must pay tribute to the officers of the Metropolitan Police whom I had dealings with that day. They had seen one of their female officer colleagues cut down in a London street by automatic gunfire and then had to escort the people responsible. They conducted themselves in the most professional manner. I know what my feelings were when I saw one of the potential offenders close up, so I can only imagine the frustration and anger some of my Met colleagues must have felt. Credit to them.

By the very nature of the type of work Support Group was asked to assist with, we did tend to see the seamier side of life. However, there were times while still required to perform high profile duties, we had the chance to enjoy ourselves, meet nice ordinary members of the public and be seen as regular police officers.

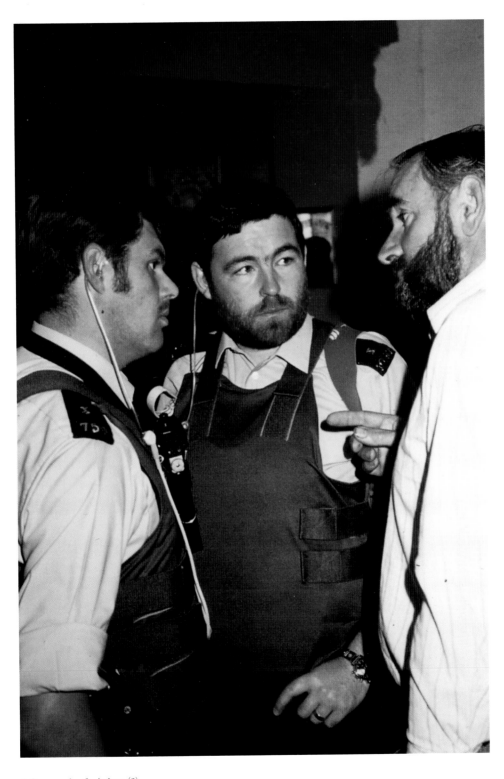

A few words of wisdom (2)

Opposite: They were only pulling his leg (4) Above - Top: Christmas Day with the Prime Minister (5)
Bottom: Meeting a hero (6)

Above: She is around here somewhere (7) Opposite: And sometimes they kneel at your feet (8)

Opposite - Top: Me as a sergeant on the Support Group with my team in 1984. We asked if we could test drive the 'vehicle' in the photo! Actually we were performing duty at the Greenham Common Air Show. It was an enjoyable duty and made a pleasant change (9) Bottom: My team prior to starting a search near Reading (10) Above: Part of my team preparing for a night patrol (11) Below: Just a little light refreshment (12)

Opposite: Inspector in charge of 'my' station, Gerrards Cross (13) Above: First day back on Support Group as Inspector (14)

Plotting the area to be searched (15)

The scene of the search at the Pig Farm (16)

Petrol bomb exploding
against the riot shield (17)

Above: There are three police officers with shields behind that blaze (18) Opposite: During the search at the Pig Farm murder near Maidenhead. A friend and colleague PF and me (19)

Fingertip search at murder scene, High Wycombe 1987 (20)

CHAPTER 10

—

Searches

Investigating a mystery

I have made several references to searches at the scene of major crimes; murders, rapes, robberies and missing persons etc. It is a highly specialised skill to conduct a search correctly. The basics were the same whether it was a line search in open country looking for a missing person or a suspect, sometimes armed, or a detailed fingertip search as referred to elsewhere. There were certain rules to be followed in all circumstances. One imperative was that once we had been given the brief of what was required, what the parameters were and of course what we were searching for, we as the searchers were in charge of that search. There was also one other in-house rule which we instigated. When we arrived and got changed into our search clothing, we would not commence the search until after we had had a team photograph taken. There was normally a scene of crime officer (SOCO) present and we would insist on photo first then search. The SOCOs soon became used to the fact that they were responsible for taking the photographs of my team posing before we got down to the business in hand.

Of all the work we were required to get involved in, the one area that we disliked the most and probably found the most difficult was where offences occurred involving children. One such case which never went away centred around Wokingham, Berkshire in June 1984. It was originally for a missing seven year old boy, Mark Tildesley. Mark had gone to the fairground nearby to where he lived in Wokingham and when he had not returned by 9.00pm, his mum and dad went to look for him. All they found was his bicycle chained to the gates at the fairground.

He had not returned by the next morning and we were called in to conduct a search of the area. We commenced a search of the immediate area and then moved on to the house to house enquiries. After a week there was still no sign of Mark or any substantial evidence of what had happened to him. There were by now a large number of officers working full time on the enquiry. By the second weekend we were no further forward, so for the Saturday and Sunday we organised and supervised a search which went further afield. We were assisted by over one hundred soldiers from the REME regiment at nearby Arborfield Garrison. By the end of the weekend we had covered more than twenty five miles, but still found no clues as to the whereabouts of Mark.

The main thrust of the investigation related to the suspicion that he had been abducted and enquiries were geared in that direction. We took possession of a caravan in a field near to where the fair had been held, it having moved on the day after Mark went missing. We made a detailed search of the caravan but it revealed nothing. A man working at the fair was traced to Cornwall and interviewed but again we were no further forward. After a number of weeks our involvement in the enquiry was scaled down and we returned to our normal duties, whilst always thinking about poor Mark and what had happened to him.

The investigation never closed, and enquiries continued in a certain direction. After six years we did have more of an idea of what had happened. Owing to a great deal of tenacious investigative work by a special team including a Detective Superintendent from TVP, there were convictions for related offences. In 1992 a paedophile was given two life sentences for his role in the killing of Mark at a sickening homosexual orgy. At his trial he admitted manslaughter and a serious sexual offence. Three youngsters are known to have been killed by this man and his associates and he was already serving sentences for the deaths of the other two. Detectives involved in this operation, named Operation Orchid, are convinced that the toll was very much higher. A total of four men were jailed in 1989. The full scale of the atrocities committed by this man and his group of associates will probably never fully emerge.

We do know some of what happened to Mark when he was abducted from the fairground that evening in 1984, but he has never been found nor his body discovered. It is more than thirty years since Mark went missing but it never goes away. When I hear on the news that a body has been found I am immediately back at Wokingham and I think, 'this is it, they have found Mark's body'. Regrettably that is not so and to date it has not happened. One day, perhaps.

During 1984 one of the main issues on a national scale was the miners' strike, which featured policing on a massive scale mainly in Yorkshire and Nottinghamshire. All police forces in England and Wales supplied police officers by mutual aid, to assist where required to deal with the strike. Owing to the nature of Support Group duties, primary function being the tactical firearms team, we were not allowed to leave the TVP area and so did not get involved in the miners' strike for long periods or together as a team. We were allowed to travel with the TVP contingent, but only one or two of us at a time and we normally fulfilled the job of quartermaster, taking the riot equipment for distribution as and when it was required.

It was a very difficult time for all concerned, not least the miners! In policing terms, it was dealt with in TVP by sending a number of PSUs. They worked away for one week, went back to their home stations for two weeks then away again for another week and so on. To backfill while the PSUs were away for their week, all officers back in TVP were working twelve hour shifts to cover for the losses. The strike lasted for more than twelve months and it was a watershed in certain aspects of policing on a large scale.

One evening in July 1984, we were working a 1800 – 0200 hours shift, assisting Milton Keynes police area with crime patrols; it had been a fairly uneventful tour of duty. I debriefed my team at 0100 and we left to return to our home stations. I was travelling with one of my team, who I was to drop off at Aylesbury. We had just stopped in Aylesbury to check out a couple of people and were about to go off duty, when the control room called me and the team to attend Edlesborough village as a matter of urgency. It was about ten miles away, near to the Bedfordshire and Hertfordshire border. When we arrived in the village there was a great deal of police activity and I was met by armed officers from Bedfordshire Police. This was most unusual. We were more aware than most that armed police do not go into another police force area with guns, unless it was something urgent or totally unavoidable. I was not a happy bunny. We were in the TVP area and if armed officers were present it should be us and not officers from another force, albeit from next door in Bedfordshire. I found the senior officer present and demanded to know what officers from elsewhere were doing patrolling with guns IN MY ******* POLICE AREA.

I contacted my control room to make sure that they were aware because I wasn't until I arrived. I was then briefed about an ongoing operation which was being run from Dunstable, Bedfordshire, which could have had the most serious consequences. We were vaguely aware that an operation had been running in Bedfordshire and Hertfordshire, but did not know any details until then.

Some weeks earlier a burglary had occurred in Bedfordshire where a shotgun and ammunition had been stolen. A man had been badly assaulted in the ensuing attack. Other burglaries had taken place in the area surrounding Leighton Buzzard, believed to be by the same offender. A man had been shot and in another incident a man had been forced to tie up his wife. He was then bound and made to watch whilst she was raped. These brutal attacks had continued which was why Bedfordshire Police were engaged in armed patrols close to our border.

Around 11pm a woman in the village of Edlesborough heard noises inside the house downstairs. Her husband got up, put lights on and looking out of the bedroom window, saw a man outside their open kitchen window with a shotgun under his arm. Clearly putting the lights on had disturbed him and he made off. Officers involved in the operation had responded and began searching the area. The operation was named Operation Peanut because in one of the offenders' early attacks he had taken food, including packets of peanuts and eaten them whilst still in the house. He had also built a lair or a hide, sometimes out of chairs and blankets inside the houses he raided. For that reason, he had been dubbed by the press as The Fox.

After a detailed briefing we supplemented the patrols for several hours, but there were no sightings or tracks. There was nothing to indicate where the offender had gone when he had been disturbed. Then things changed dramatically.

We had reached the point when we were considering calling off the search, when it was discovered that three young people had been held hostage in a house near to the last sighting of him. It was clear that he had been holed up there whilst the search had been going on nearby. It transpired that he had broken in to the house where an eighteen year old girl, her boyfriend and her brother had been staying whilst their parents were away. During the hours that we were looking for him he had tied them up, raped the girl and committed serious depraved sexual assaults on all of them. He had then left them tied up while he made his escape. After some time, they had managed to free themselves. Again, a comprehensive search of the area failed to locate him. By lunchtime the next day, we were relieved by the day turn Support Group teams and we returned home.

I was called at home later that day to be told that as of 6.00pm we would be engaged in armed patrols in the same area that we had been searching the previous evening. I met with my team on Edlesborough village green which we had taken over as our base. Our duties followed the normal pattern under such circumstances; two parties of Support Group would work twelve hours out on plot, 1800 to 0600 hours and be relieved by the two remaining parties who would work twelve hours day turn. This would remain until further notice. Those shifts would be continuous armed patrols, acting as a deterrent as well as in readiness to respond to any sightings or attacks. My first task was to attend Dunstable police station where I was directed to a church hall in the town centre for a detailed briefing for our night's patrol.

This was to be our duty for the next few weeks. There were several events which are worthy of note. Remembering that we were all overtly armed, with hand guns clearly on view and extra firepower of support weapons, such as the pump action shotguns carried by some of the team, it was most unusual or even rare to patrol in such a manner. The first evening we arrived at the village green and armed up ready for patrol, the police helicopter had already landed on the green and it was obvious that most of the village had turned out to watch. After five days, no one took any notice of the armed officers even the children, who had previously been hanging over the fence in their droves showed us no regard and were more interested in playing football.

It was said that the British public would not accept the police being armed. Well in that part of Buckinghamshire, Bedfordshire and later Hertfordshire, they accepted it very quickly. I assume it was a form of extra reassurance for the people who lived locally. By now the press was full of 'The Fox' and local people were indeed very concerned. The attacks had been going on for about ten weeks and totalled about thirty, they also became progressively worse. The concern was that, with the reckless use of the shotgun it may only have been a matter of time before someone was murdered.

On our second week of these duties, I attended Dunstable for the nightly briefing. I parked at the police station and was walking to the church hall. I was fully kitted out so that I could respond at short notice, so was already armed. As I walked past the local Sainsbury's, a man and woman were just emerging with a full shopping trolley when the man called out, "Excuse me, can I have a word?" I stopped to speak to him and fully expected him to make comment about the way I was dressed and carrying a gun. He pressed a piece of paper into my hand and said, "I live in Edlesborough with my family and we are terrified of The Fox. I sit up all night. This is my address, please call in for coffee and ask your officers to do the same anytime, you will be very welcome." That showed the high level of fear which existed at that time.

The briefing each evening was impressive. It could be difficult on a long running operation to keep up the level of interest and not let complacency creep in. That was not so for our armed patrols, but a reality for the large number of police officers out there during the night on static observations on canal paths and footpaths, where it was believed the offender made his escape. The officer in charge did a really good job at the briefings, keeping the interest high. He had been saying for some time that a lot was known about the offender, his height, build and voice. In fact, he knew pretty much everything about him except for who he was and what he looked like, because he always wore a full-face balaclava with eye slits. One evening there was a full-size cardboard cut out on the stage for the briefing. The officer in charge introduced the cut out as the offender. He said, "This is him. When you find him, he will fit into this cut out and when you find him you will know it is him. Now get out there and find him for me." Clever, inspirational and most unusual, but it generated the reaction it was supposed to.

By then we had developed a system of patrol which worked well. We had a number of our cars, all unmarked with two or three Support Group officers in each car, all armed. This was to supplement the officers out on the ground. We were aware of the location of their static points so that if any officer called anything in, we could respond immediately with armed and police dog support. We found that once things had got quiet just after 11.00pm, we could sit up at six different locations, hidden from general view and could cover all entry and exit roads to the village. We quickly got to know all the local cars, their movements and times of their comings and goings.

In the early hours of one morning around 2.00am, normally a quiet time, I received a call from one of our other cars that they had seen a vehicle come past them, a strange one that they had not seen before. We were able to track the car as it entered the village; at one point it came past my position as if leaving the area but then reappeared on the other side of the village. On two occasions it stopped, but after a couple of minutes moved off to elsewhere in the village. We could see that there were four men in the car. A registered owner check revealed that it belonged to someone in London. After watching the car circulate around the village for about ten minutes I gave the order that we would do a 'hard stop' on the car. That was blocking it front and back with officers confronting the occupants with guns drawn, but stopping short of smashing the windows and dragging them out onto the road. It worked to perfection owing to the element of surprise; they had not seen us at all. Suddenly the car was surrounded by armed officers and in one coordinated movement the doors were flung open and guns pointed at each of the occupants. To say they were shocked is a bit of an understatement and as you can imagine they were more than helpful in answering our questions. They were taken out of the car and spoken to separately. It was very obvious that they did not have a clue where they were or what was happening.

Imagine how disconcerting it must have been for them. There they were, four villains out from London to do a bit of villainy in the quiet countryside of sleepy Buckinghamshire. Not a soul about at 2 o'clock in the morning and lots of tasty properties to break into, when all of a sudden they were 'helped' out of the car by police officers pointing guns at them. Once it was pointed out to them the sensitive area they were in and the reason for our being there, they were immensely relieved. We 'turned over' the car and all the occupants thoroughly, but nothing of any note was found. We took all their details and circulated them. We pointed out in the strongest possible terms that it was not healthy for them to go mooching around the countryside after dark with armed police everywhere. They agreed collectively and I suspected that would be the last we saw of them in our neck of the woods.

The operation carried on for some weeks until two CID officers called at an address in Kentish Town, North London to interview a potential suspect. This was one of hundreds of such enquiries raised since the operation had commenced. The difference with this one was that outside the house they were calling at, was a parked vehicle similar to one believed to be used by the offender. The officers had also seen something inside the car which further raised their suspicions. The two officers have both said since that when they first saw the man they had come to interview, they both thought independently, 'This is him and we have got him'. They were right, it was. The Fox had been caught at last.

He was later charged with a number of serious offences which had taken place over many weeks running from June to August, in a triangle around Leighton Buzzard, Bedfordshire including nearby Hertfordshire and Buckinghamshire. He was convicted and sentenced to a substantial term of imprisonment. Edlesborough and its environs could at last return to normal.

Operation Janet took place at Reading in November 1984. It was one of many where we were engaged in assisting the Drug Squad and in this instance, the Regional Crime Squad. They had been working jointly on an operation involving the importation and distribution of illegal drugs, in this case vast quantities of cocaine. The reason for our involvement was twofold. Firstly, undercover police officers would be posing as drug dealers intent on buying cocaine and therefore had a large amount of money with them as 'flash money'. Secondly, with such vast quantities of high value drugs, those selling the drugs would always be armed for their protection, normally with sawn-off shotguns. Armed police protection was imperative to protect the undercover officers and ensure the security of the 'flash money'.

A meeting had been arranged to take place in a hotel room to do the deal between the drug dealers and the undercover police officers posing as local dealers intent on buying the cocaine. We were in rough civilian clothes so as not to stand out and positioned in various locations including an adjoining hotel room. Our main strike team was outside in unmarked vehicles. The meeting took place and, the 'flash money' of £50,000 cash, which we were there to protect on pain of death if we lost it, was shown to the dealers. Once they had seen that amount of money the deal was really on, it was irresistible. The drugs were in a vehicle in the outside car park and the undercover officers were invited to the car to view the goods. That having been set up and in place, the 'strike' was called and armed officers appeared from everywhere and arrested everybody in sight, including the undercover officers. It all worked superbly well; no problems, no shots fired, all the baddies arrested, firearms recovered, our £50,000 'flash money' safe and cocaine to the street value of £3 million recovered.

Shortly afterwards, everything had been sorted out at the scene. I returned to Reading police station in one of our unmarked vehicles with two of my officers. We had on board the £50,000 cash and the seized cocaine. A valuable load and a potential temptation for weaker mortals, but not for these boys.

Early on Christmas Eve morning in 1984, I was called at home to turn my team out to Denham Golf Club, where the naked body of a young woman had been found. On arrival we were informed that she had been murdered and her body dumped near to the 16th tee. Our job was to conduct a fingertip search at the location where she was found and the area leading into it. It appeared that she had been killed elsewhere and her body dumped on the golf course. I initially liaised with the golf club staff, we required an area to be taped off and out of bounds to everyone until we had completed our task. We worked nonstop, flat out without a break from early morning until late afternoon in an effort to finish before Christmas.

I reported to the golf club manager that we had completed our work and that we were returning the area back to him. He told us that he had been very busy with a Christmas party, that was now finished and he enquired if we had eaten or had anything to drink. As we hadn't, he very kindly invited us into the golf club for some refreshments which were gratefully received. The staff were fascinated by their unusual uniformed guests who were partaking of some festive cheer. I was able to locate and take possession of the Polaroid photographs to ensure that none appeared later to cause us any grief.

It was discovered that the victim was a regular peace protester at the Greenham Common protest camp. The unusual and bizarre circumstances of how the murder was solved were almost beyond belief. The young lady was hitching a lift in London, eventually a car stopped, the driver offered her a lift and she got in. This was witnessed by a member of the public, a man standing at a nearby bus stop. He was slightly perplexed by this young woman hitching a lift. Shortly before he had seen a TV programme warning about the possible dangers of young people accepting lifts from strangers in cars. With this in mind as the scene unfolded in front of him, he thought how unwise it was for this young lady to get into a stranger's car, so he made a note of the registration number, the colour and make of the car. When he later read of the discovery of the body of a young woman he rang his local police and reported what he had seen. They passed this information to the TVP murder incident room and an enquiry was raised for the registered owner of the car to be visited. It transpired that he was the driver at the time and further detailed questioning revealed that it was he who had committed the murder. The police found evidence at his home address which had been taken from the victim. You just could not make it up. If that had been the plot for some television detective programme it would not be believable and yet it was all true.

CHAPTER 11

—

All in a Day's Work

An outsider

This chronicled one day's duty while I was a Support Group sergeant, although I must say it was not typical. It was September 1986.

0800 hours - On duty, travelled from home address to the training centre at Sulhamstead, near Reading. There was a senior officers' firearms seminar on Friday and we were to perform a demonstration of an armed robbery; an attack on a security van. We needed to practice to get it right.

0930 hours – Sulhamstead. Briefed with two Support Group parties, eighteen of us and sorted out the roles we were to play. These were the two parties from the southern end of the force and I was a sergeant on a northern party, but someone had to work with the southern boys!

1010 hours – While still preparing, a call came in for us to attend nearby Wallingford where a man armed with a crossbow was at large, having shot two people with crossbow bolts and threatened several more. I deployed with some of my officers and we located him almost immediately. He was threatening to shoot with the crossbow and we did not have our firearms, they had been requested but were still on the way. It was a dangerous situation and if we had been armed we would have challenged him at gunpoint. As we did not have that facility we adapted and improvised. We told him to put the crossbow and bolts on the ground; he refused so we ran him over with the Landover instead. He wasn't badly injured and he was arrested and taken away.

1100 hours – Back at Sulhamstead, we resumed our practice. We were a bit short of personnel now with some still involved at the scene in Wallingford. Others were with the prisoner, so I played the role of a villain and got arrested three times for armed robbery before lunch.

1230 hours – A nice leisurely lunch at the training centre after an interesting morning.

1330 hours – Departed for Reading police station.

1400 hours – Arrived at the incident room in Reading. We were already involved with house to house enquiries in two areas of Reading, where two separate rapes had taken place. I received a request from the officer in charge of the enquiry to arrange for a detailed search to take place the next day at one of the scenes. Scene visited, and arrangements made for the search tomorrow.

1600 hours – One more party of Support Group arrived, Party 4, that was my team of officers and I briefed them for the house to house enquiries to be done.

1615 hours – I left Reading to drive to the police headquarters at Kidlington, near Oxford, with one of my officers.

1715 hours – At HQ with my police constable who was to be interviewed by one of the Assistant Chief Constables (ACC). It was not really an interview, it was a bollocking for him for a slight error of judgement he had made. Fingers crossed for him whilst he was with the ACC.

1730 hours – While at HQ, I firmed up arrangements for the change of duty the next day regarding the search at the scene of the rape at Reading and ensured that the van with all our specialist search equipment was made ready and available.

1830 hours – My PC's interview with the ACC had finished and he was in the clear, having received 'advice'. We departed Kidlington and returned to Reading for the house to house enquiries.

1930 hours – Reading police station, meal break.

2030 hours – In our Support Group office, I sorted through the house to house enquiry forms completed by our officers.

2200 hours – I'd had enough for the day and departed Reading for home.

2230 hours – Approximately half way home and I got a call on the radio. There had been a murder at Marlow. I was very near, so I called in to the police station to see if they required anything from us. Thankfully it appeared to be all sorted so there was nothing for us at that time. We would contact them again the next day to see if the situation remained the same.

2235 hours – Five minutes later! A call from the police HQ control room, an urgent request, for us to make for the prison, HMP Grendon Underwood, between Aylesbury and Bicester. A hostage situation was developing. That was two tones and blue lights all the way.

2255 hours – Arrived HMP Grendon Underwood. ACC Operations, who I had seen earlier with my PC, Detective Chief Superintendent, Chief Superintendent from Aylesbury, our boss (the Chief Inspector) and the local bobby for the village were all in attendance. That shows that it must have been serious for the local bobby to be there at that time of night!

2335 hours – By now all my team had arrived and having been briefed on the current situation we were told that it was all in hand. We were not required so we stood down to return to our home addresses.

2355 hours – Whilst we were all making our way to our homes, there was a 10-9 call on the radio. This was not used very often; it was only ever called by an officer when he/she was in urgent need of assistance or in grave danger. This call came from an ex Support Group colleague in Aylesbury, who used to be on my team. We all knew him very well and he would not normally require any assistance, so it must have been serious. I had one of my PCs with me who I was dropping off at home, so we diverted to the address given and were first to arrive. After a violent struggle a man was arrested for criminal damage, resisting arrest and assault on police, after he had thrown our ex-colleague down the stairs. Two more of my team arrived shortly after and took the prisoner to Aylesbury police station. Back at the station the prisoner bit one of my officers and once in his cell, smashed it up. On checking him we found that he was a homosexual transvestite and a drug addict with a bad habit. AND HE HAD BITTEN ONE OF MY MEN! We were concerned for our bitten colleague, Graham, whose nickname was Don. The rest of the team 'reassured' him by telling him that he may have been infected with AIDS and/or Hepatitis or worse!

0115 hours – We took Don straight to Stoke Mandeville Hospital to have his bum pumped full of penicillin. Unbeknown to him the nurses let one of our team listen in the next cubicle. He came back and blabbed to all of us what a wimp Don had been!

0150 hours – We were all on our way home again when we got a call that there had been a smash and grab at Gerrards Cross. Sod it, unless it was desperate we would pass on this one. I was knackered and made my way home.

0200 hours – Home and bed, wonderful, what a day zzzzzzzzzzzzzz

0335 hours – F*** me, it couldn't be, the bloody phone was ringing! It was that nice inspector from the HQ's control room. The wheel had come off at the prison and my team were to be called out to go straight there.

0338 hours – The phones were red hot as I called them all out again. "Get up you lazy bastards you've had at least an hour in bed, what more do you want?"

0430 hours – Arrived HMP Grendon Underwood

0500 hours – We were briefed by the ACC Operations AND the Deputy Chief Constable, now that was unusual. There was then a bit of an inquisition by them to discuss our capability of achieving a quick entry into a prison cell. It was a bit like a promotion board being quizzed by those two. The current situation was that a prisoner was holding another prisoner hostage in his cell and threatening to kill him. We were taking his threat seriously.

0635 hours – We moved to Aylesbury police station to standby whilst another of our Support Group teams was on standby at the prison. We formulated plans and went over the details.

1210 hours – Lunchtime the next day, WE WERE STILL THERE! On duty 28 hours 10 minutes so far and counting.

1300 hours – My team and I were now relieved by the other northern Support Group party and we were stood down to return home for much needed sleep.

1330 hours – Home and bed. PHEW! Not a normal day, but an unforgettable one. At least I had the rest of the day off to do whatever I wanted!

There is something called the European Working Time Directive which limits the amount of time workers are allowed to be at work each day and week. Not sure how this would fit in!

CHAPTER 12

—

Prison Hostage Siege

Police court jailer

The prison hostage siege was still ongoing when we returned to work, so it became the main priority until it was resolved. On reporting to the prison, we were fully apprised of the current situation and what led up to it. Grendon Underwood was a Category B establishment and contained an average of two hundred and sixty inmates. Some of those were long term psychiatric prisoners. The hostage taker was undergoing psychiatric assessment. He was serving a lengthy term of imprisonment for serious offences. Previously at a different prison, he had taken two prisoners hostage and threatened their lives with a razor blade. That incident was peacefully concluded after three days. He received a further term of imprisonment for those offences.

At about 7.30pm on the Wednesday evening, prison officers were informed that an inmate was lying unconscious in a recess area on the first floor. When they found him, he was out cold and displaying signs of advanced strangulation. Normal prison procedures were immediately introduced which was a lock down; all prisoners were returned to their cells and a roll call taken. All prisoners except one were accounted for. The staff then began to open each cell, but when they came to the hostage takers cell they found it had been barricaded with the bed and they couldn't get in. The prisoner asked the prison officers if they had found his 'present', referring to the unconscious prisoner. From what he said, he believed that he had killed the other prisoner.

He told the staff that he had another prisoner in his cell; they could see this person on the floor, apparently unconscious. He said that he would kill his hostage with the broken sauce bottle that he brandished in front of them. He then attacked the other prisoner kicking him in the head. The bed used as a barricade, had been firmly fixed behind the door in such a way that it left only four inches for it to open. He said that if prison officers tried to use their door-opening apparatus he would have plenty of time to kill his hostage. He had that knowledge from his previous experience of hostage taking. The remaining prisoners were cleared from the wing and TVP were called.

The options available were those constant in all hostage situations.

(i) Negotiation to bring about a peaceful solution.

(ii) Affect entry into the stronghold, in this case a cell with a solid door and barred windows, to secure the safe release of the hostage.

There was no contest at that early stage and the decision was made to pursue the course of negotiation for as long as possible and work for a peaceful resolution. In the meantime, the role of the Support Group supervisors was to examine the tactical options available and formulate an entry plan should it become necessary, in an attempt to release the hostage.

The problems readily identified in relation to executing a hostage release raid were:

Limited access. There was just one door which was solid and two inches thick. Access was gained to this door along a fairly narrow corridor.

The window comprised small panes separated by bars, thus making target identification from outside very difficult. It made the introduction of CS gas, via a12 bore ferret fired from a shotgun, even more tricky. The hostage taker had masked the window with what appeared to be a blanket, further exacerbating the problem.

The walls connecting the cells were constructed of engineering bricks and special mortar. This limited the possibility of gaining access to the cell via the wall from the adjoining cell.

The door was made of solid two inch thick wood. This, coupled with the narrow corridor, made the introduction of CS gas through the closed door too hazardous to contemplate.

The device used by the prison service to force open doors, whilst very efficient was extremely slow, taking in the region of six to eight minutes to affect entry. This obviously allowed the hostage taker far too much time to injure or kill his hostage.

Finally, as mentioned previously, the hostage taker had done this before and was aware at all times of the steps likely to be considered by the prison authorities and the police.

The plan formulated to gain entry into the cell had to acknowledge the fact that we could not guarantee the speedy removal of the door. Any delay would give the hostage taker the opportunity to carry out his threat to cut the hostage's throat. The primary function of a cell was to keep prisoners in and not to allow them to break out. In this case the reverse applied; it was difficult to break into, especially with speed and urgency.

Several weeks prior to this incident a door opening device had been demonstrated to TVP. It had been used on a locked and bolted door and was seen to break it open in three seconds. The manufacturers maintained at the time of the demonstration that the device, working on hydraulic pressure, would do the same to a cell door. During the Thursday, Merseyside Police, who had purchased one of these devices, were contacted and asked if it could be made available to us. We were later informed that two officers from their drug squad were on route to us with the door opening device. They arrived in the evening and by then we had updated our plan.

The TVP ACC asked whether in our opinion, the safe release of the hostage could be attained without the use of CS gas. The answer was emphatically, "No". We felt that without the CS gas we had no chance of effecting entry quickly enough to prevent the hostage being injured or killed. The use of CS gas would therefore be authorised if the plan needed to be implemented. The plan was as follows;

Two snipers, each armed with a Remington pump action shotgun loaded with CS gas ferret cartridges, were placed on standby at the corner of the cell block in the exercise yard.

Three officers would be placed on standby near an adjoining cell.

Five officers under the control of the Support Group inspector, would be on standby in the corridor around the corner from the stronghold cell.

Three prison officers of the MUFTI Squad (Minimum Use of Force Tactical Intervention), who were specially trained in cell entry techniques and control and restraint tactics for use in penal establishments, introduced in 1978, would also be placed on standby around the corner in the cell corridor.

All officers, including the prison staff, would be wearing respirators. We gave the prison officers a crash course in the use of these and they practised putting them on and getting used to wearing them.

On being given the instruction to enter the stronghold, the Support Group inspector would count down and give the instruction to go.

The two snipers would run from the corner of the cell block into the yard and fire one ferret cartridge each into the upper panes of the window. This was to ensure that the missiles would go directly into the ceiling and not injure either of the occupants of the cell. Simultaneously two officers would run from the standby point with the door opener and operate it on the cell door.

Also simultaneously two officers, each equipped with a sledge hammer, would enter the cell adjacent to the stronghold cell and attack the connecting wall with the sledges. This would serve two purposes, firstly, to act as a diversion and to try to keep the hostage taker's mind occupied for the two or three seconds that it would take for the CS gas to become effective. Secondly, it would eventually provide an alternative means of access should the door not come off quickly enough.

At the same time, one officer was to run from the same place with a small spike axe to smash the glass in the spy hole in the door, to enable the introduction of CS gas from an aerosol. This was to provide complete saturation of the cell as we believed the window being covered by a blanket would absorb some of the irritant from the CS gas ferrets.

Immediately after this course of action described, three of the five officers and the inspector would run from their standby position in the corridor and spray CS gas through the spy hole and/or through the door, which we hoped would be partially open by then. Together with the remaining two officers, they would enter the cell and remove the hostage. If possible the prison officers of the MUFTI Squad would take care of the hostage taker. If there were any problems there were sufficient officers in close proximity to deal with any eventuality.

During the course of the Thursday and Friday, the officers involved were briefed and re-briefed. Throughout this period various crises occurred in the stronghold with the hostage being beaten and tortured. As each crisis arrived the team donned respirators and stood in readiness to execute the plan, standing down as the crisis passed. The Support Group teams were relieved on a twelve-hour basis. The hydraulic door opener had been tested on an identical cell door with a bed barricade. Happily, it worked, taking the door off its hinges in approximately four seconds.

Friday morning was a repeat performance of Thursday, with the same crises coming and going as threats and repeated demands were made. Shortly after midday, the hostage taker shouted that he had beaten the hostage until he was unconscious, and he had gouged out one of his eyes. That was it. We took up our standby positions and awaited instructions. We were then informed that the hostage had been hung upside down from the ceiling light fitting. One officer in the line-up was nominated to deal with the hostage taker and his broken bottle on entry into the cell. The second officer was nominated to lift the hostage and take his weight whilst he was cut down from his suspended position. The MUFTI Squad were asked to remain outside the cell until we had secured it.

At 1327 hours on Friday 17th October the prison hierarchy handed over and signed authority for the police to act, a requisite for legal reasons. We then got the authority to go from the ACC. The countdown and instruction to 'Go' was given over the radio to all officers. The two snipers ran into position and fired. The two officers with the door opener ran forward. They placed the machine in position and operated it. The spy glass was smashed and CS gas was sprayed into the aperture. By this time the door had started to collapse inwards and more gas was sprayed in through the gap. Throughout those few seconds, the two officers with the sledge hammers had started hammering on the connecting wall. The bottom of the door, which was now off, was jammed against the bed. It was lifted and thrown into the cell. The team entered the cell and found the hostage taker crouched in a foetal position in the corner. The hostage was lying on the floor half under the bed and apparently unconscious. The hostage was removed and handed over to the ambulance service. The prison officers dealt with the hostage taker, he had been totally incapacitated by the CS gas and offered no resistance at all.

Our debrief showed the reason the hostage was found on the floor. When the cell door came off its hinges, it had hit his legs and pulled him off the light fitting causing him to fall. The distraction team had done a superb job. On examination of the adjoining wall, they had almost completely broken through.

It could be suggested that too much CS gas was used, but we went for the option which we felt was most likely to succeed and that included total and instant saturation. It worked. The hostage suffered a sore head and he had been systematically cut with broken glass over the course of two days. However, he did not die or get his throat cut so the plan was successful.

This operation was ground breaking in a number of ways, not least with the use of the CS gas. It was the first time that it had been used in a prison on the British mainland. We also had the use of the new hydraulic door opener which proved invaluable. In fact, we were so enamoured with it we acquired one soon after for our own use.

The hostage taker later appeared before the Crown Court and was sentenced to several life sentences to run concurrently.

CHAPTER 13

—

Initiation Ceremony

A smart capture

In keeping with many other careers new members of staff, new probationary police constables in this case, were sometimes subjected to an initiation ceremony. Whilst I was with Support Group we were asked occasionally to assist local officers in taking part in such 'ceremonies'. This was mainly because we were from outside of the shift involved and we were not known by everyone. It normally took place in the dead of night when it was quiet and nothing much was happening.

We assisted one night at Slough with a new woman police constable (WPC) of only a few weeks service. At that time The Two Ronnies were very popular on TV with their comedy series, which included a regular sketch called The Phantom Raspberry Blower of Old London Town. We replicated this at 3.00am in the pedestrianised Slough High Street when the female officer resumed her foot patrol after her meal break. When she was at the far end of the High Street, one of my officers, now dressed in rough civilian clothes, came out into the High Street about a hundred yards away from her. He shouted to her, blew a raspberry and called out, "Here I want a word with you," as per The Two Ronnies sketch. As she hurried towards him, he dived back into the shadows. She had almost reached him when a second officer, dressed almost identically, came out from behind the shops where she had started from. This officer did exactly the same calling, "Here I want a word with you," and blew a raspberry. She of course turned and ran back up the High Street towards him. This went on about four times.

Those of us watching from a safe concealed distance with the remainder of her colleagues could see her becoming more and more confused, then she eventually called up on the radio for some help. The control room were also in on the joke and made some excuse that it would take a few minutes to get some assistance to her. She gave it one more go before she realised something was not right here and wouldn't play anymore. At that point everyone came out of hiding and congratulated her on her perseverance and fitness, although she was sweating a bit by now. She took it all in good part and when the two 'raspberry blowers' appeared and got close enough she thumped the pair of them. Fair play to her.

Another time we were asked to assist at one of the biggest stations in TVP. This joke had been used several times and involved a newly appointed constable who was asked to take part in playing a practical joke on someone from their station, ignorant of the fact that the joke was to be played on him. The new recruit was to be taken to the local mortuary during a quiet time in the middle of the night. With the mortuary assistant's help, he was to be laid in one of the body drawers, unaware that there was already another colleague in an adjacent drawer covered with a sheet. After a while the second person says, "Its cold in here." Thus giving the new constable the fright of his life. They always used an area which was completely empty, no bodies were involved.

In this instance the joke was reversed and played on one of the older members of the shift, not the most popular officer on the station. He was a bit grumpy and initially said that he didn't hold with such nonsense and refused. He was told that he was needed for the initiation of the new boy because he knew how it worked. Eventually, with reluctance, he agreed and it was set up.

The mortuary assistant met the grumpy PC, let him in, dressed him in a white robe and helped him onto one of the sliding drawer cabinets. When the mortuary assistant said that the sergeant and the new boy had arrived, the drawer was closed. As the grumpy one lay there in the dark waiting for his cue the 'body' next to him said, "Its cold in here ain't it?" It was of course a spoof on the grumpy one for being such a miserable git to everyone. Needless to say, he didn't see the funny side of it. In fact, he flew out of the drawer screaming his head off. The 'body' next to him was his sergeant, who obviously thought it was a really good wheeze.

These spoof games do not always go as planned and we heard of one where it did not end well, fortunately we were not involved. The night shift had arranged in the dead of night for a 'struggle' to take place on the roof of the shopping centre between one of the officers and a dummy. The officer on the roof called for assistance and the new young probationary constable, who was nearby, responded. What he saw on arrival was his colleague, the officer on the roof, struggling with the 'offender' i.e. the dummy. They were near the edge of the roof and he saw the 'offender' slip from the officer's grasp and fall from the roof. Other officers quickly removed the dummy and when the sergeant arrived he told both officers not to say anything because, 'the inspector would sort it all out'. The problem was that the new young officer was, perhaps not surprisingly, upset enough to contact the superintendent to say that he was resigning because his colleagues had killed someone! Suffice it to say that there was a dressing down for all concerned and it was the end of that initiation ceremony. The intended resignation was withdrawn.

CHAPTER 14

–

Promotion

Divisional inspector of police

Eventually the time came to stop enjoying myself as a sergeant with Support Group and get back to the real world of policing. I was very fortunate in May 1987 to be promoted to inspector and be posted to Amersham. It was unusual for me to be working so close to where I lived. I found the transition from sergeant to inspector a little strange to begin with. The sergeant drives the officers on and designates their duties for patrol as well as directing operations out on the streets. The inspector's role was more of an overview offering advice and guidance to the sergeant and the officers, when and where and if it was required. Very early on, I had a detailed discussion with my patrol sergeant at Amersham about the shift of officers, their strengths and weaknesses etc... I also told him that I would need time to get used to my new job and if he ever felt that I was impinging on his role then he must tell me so. I found that my duties as an inspector in the police station didn't take very long so as soon as I could I took a car out to supplement the patrolling officers.

That first week, late at night, there was a call reporting a fight at the local chip shop. I attended with several of my officers and discovered that a knife had been used and someone had been stabbed. I was pretty sure who had the knife and who had been involved. Together, with one of the officers reputed to be good operationally, we took this individual to one side, found the knife and arrested him. By now there were several other 'customers' full of drink who were busting to get arrested. We accommodated them and finished up with it all sorted and several in custody. A good result. As we were resuming I saw my sergeant looking at me as if he wanted to say something. It then dawned on me and I said, "I have just done what I said I wasn't going to, haven't I?" He agreed, quite rightly. I had just taken on the sergeant's role which was out of order. I apologised and assured him I would try harder to make sure I didn't do it again.

My time as a patrol inspector at Amersham quickly settled into a pattern of shift work, early turn, late turn and nights. After only a short time I found the role not as demanding as I had imagined. That was mainly because the area covered by Amersham was much less busy in policing terms than I had been used to working with Support Group. Despite that I enjoyed my new role and it gave me the chance to explore new things not previously open to me at a rank below inspector level. It was also an opportunity to recharge my batteries. There were virtually no call outs from home, very few telephone calls whilst off duty and less requirement to work long hours. However, there were exceptions.

Saturday 13th June 1987, was the day of the Chesham Schools Carnival. This was an annual event, attended by families, held on The Moor in Chesham, a large grassed area of common land. Children from local schools and businesses took part in the procession of floats through the town to amass at the main carnival site. I was the duty inspector working 1400 – 2200 hours. Local police officers were supplemented by members of the special constabulary to help police the event. At 4.00pm I received a call for assistance from officers at the carnival. I attended immediately and found a scene of utter chaos. Outside a pub, which backed onto The Moor, a group of between one hundred and one hundred and fifty adolescents had gathered and were egging on a small group of four or five other youths, who were fighting. Officers were attempting to control the situation and stop the fights. I assisted the officers and helped break up a number of separate fights and told those involved to move away. From my previous public disorder experience, especially with Support Group, under those circumstances if people are told to do something they either do it or they are arrested. I gave them this option, told them what would happen if they didn't comply with my instructions, but all I got in reply was swearing, threats and verbal abuse. All the time this was going on parents were trying to get their children away from the melee, the brawling, the screaming and the shouting.

I was aware my officers had arrested someone, but then a crowd jumped them and freed the offender. The officers, totally outnumbered, were attempting to calm the situation. A lot of the crowd had clearly been drinking for some hours and it was getting out of hand. I told my officers to make arrests if it was possible. I saw one man who was totally out of control, shouting and screaming abuse and he threw a glass at one of the officers. I took hold of him, arrested him but as I started to take him away he lost it completely and tried to bite me. I used reasonable force to restrain him which meant grabbing his hair, wrenching his head back away from me and together with assistance from another colleague, removed him to a police vehicle. I quickly returned to continue assisting my officers. Another call for assistance resulted in support from High Wycombe and Aylesbury as well as our local CID. Eventually things calmed down, the situation was under control and the crowd dispersed.

Once order had been restored a quick debrief showed that we had arrested fifteen people, including several females, for public disorder offences and assault. Some police personnel had received injuries including me, four required treatment. The officers together with those of the special constabulary had done a magnificent job. They responded brilliantly under the most difficult and trying of circumstances and emerged with great credit. The outbreak of disorder was totally unexpected and cast a shadow over the whole proceedings. It should have been and had been for many years, a really good fun day out for families and children. As a consequence, the start of the next year's carnival was brought forward to the morning and it continued that way for some years.

Policing in Chesham and Amersham was supposed to be a quiet affair where nothing much happened, so they told me. This event proved that there were exceptions.

HUNGERFORD

Wednesday 19th August 1987 – I was performing a 1000–1800 hours duty to cover some of the early turn and the first half of the late turn. It was early afternoon and I was out on patrol in a marked police vehicle in the Amersham area. Listening to messages on the VHF radio in the car, I became aware that something untoward was happening, somewhere else in the force area. When there was a lull in radio traffic I contacted the control room, having spent all that time on Support Group I knew a lot of the radio operators especially the supervisors, sergeants and inspectors, and I wondered if there was anything I could do to help.

The message I received was chilling, words I never wanted to hear, an officer down. A tragic event was unfolding in a quiet Berkshire town. A man had gone on the rampage shooting and killing several people in Hungerford, including a police officer. That was the worst-case scenario; it was what we trained for as firearms officers but hoped and prayed that it would never happen. It was taking place in one of the most out-of-the-way locations of the TVP area, close to the Berkshire/Wiltshire border. I sat for some time absorbing the information and planning in my mind what needed to be done, although it was nothing to do with me any more. It was only three months since I had left that type of work and my ex team would be making their way to Hungerford. I was going through in my mind all the requirements, equipment needed, deployments, options and numerous other things which ten years of training and operational experience had left me with. Before I realised it I found myself driving down the A404 Marlow bypass approaching the M4 motorway and on my way to Hungerford. I was not required that day, but I was asked to attend Hungerford the next day with a number of other officers to assist in the aftermath.

It transpired that the gunman, Michael Ryan, a local man, had shot thirty two people. Seventeen of them died, including his own mother and police constable Roger Brereton, who was in his traffic patrol car. Finally, Michael Ryan committed suicide by shooting himself.

It started at the Savernake Forest in Wiltshire, seven miles to the west of Hungerford. There he shot and killed a young mother picnicking in the woods with her two young children, who were fortunately unharmed. He drove back towards Hungerford but stopped at a petrol station on the way. After filling the car and two cans with petrol, he fired several shots at the woman cashier. Luckily, she was not hit and was unharmed.

Shortly after, there were reports of shootings in the Southview area of Hungerford. Ryan had apparently returned to his home in Southview. It appears that he collected a quantity of ammunition and now had three guns, but on returning to his car it wouldn't start. He then left the car and started the shooting spree. He shot the family dog and set fire to his house using the petrol from the cans, before shooting dead two of his neighbours; a husband and wife who were in their garden.

The police were beginning to arrive and police constable Roger Brereton drove his traffic car into Southview. Ryan had walked towards the common shooting and injuring two women and then shooting dead a man who was walking with his son, before doubling back to Southview. He fired a number of shots at the police car, hitting Roger Brereton several times. Roger managed to call for help on his car radio but died soon afterwards. Ryan then walked round the police car systematically shooting; it later transpired that the police vehicle had been hit with twenty-four bullets. Ryan's mother appeared in Southview and told him to stop it. His response was to shoot her dead. His shooting and killing spree continued for a little while longer as the police attempted to locate him.

It ended with him being found in the John O'Gaunt School, it being contained by armed officers. Dialogue with him commenced. What a blessing that the school was closed at that time owing to the summer holidays, so no children were present. Attempts to negotiate a peaceful conclusion failed, even though he was talking to the police. At 6.52pm he shot himself. He was in possession of a Kalashnikov AK47 automatic rifle, an M1 Carbine and a 9mm Beretta pistol, as well as various other military type articles and equipment. He had discharged more than 119 rounds on his killing spree.

It was a day that anyone involved in any way would never forget. My thoughts and sympathy were, and still are, with the victims, their families and the people of Hungerford. Consideration should also be given to the police officers and other emergency services personnel who had to deal with unimaginable trauma. The way in which firearms incidents are dealt with would never quite be the same after this.

In September 1987, I had been at Amersham as a patrol inspector for only four months when I was given a wonderful opportunity, to move to Gerrards Cross as the inspector in charge of the station and sector. This was an unusual posting for someone of the rank of inspector. I jumped at the chance and took over from the previous inspector, a friend of mine, Roger Young.

One of my first tasks eventually proved to be an absolute pleasure and delight. Some weeks before I started at Gerrards Cross, a burglary had taken place in Chalfont St Peter, at the home of an eighty-two-year-old lady living alone. She had been saving for some time to buy a new washing machine and was devastated when the £165 she had saved was stolen.

At about the same time, Roger was notified that prior to an international football match at Wembley, involving a Rest of The World XI, the entire squad would be staying at The Bellhouse Hotel, Beaconsfield. This was on the patch of Gerrards Cross police station. A football was bought and through contacts, it was taken to the hotel to be autographed by the World XI squad. It was then handed on to Alan Parry the TV commentator, also the Wycombe Wanderers press officer. He took the football to a Wycombe Wanderers sportsmen's dinner to be auctioned. I was fortunate enough to see the ball and handle it after it had been signed by Gary Lineker, Michel Platini, Diego Maradona and many more. What a marvellous job Alan did. People such as ex Arsenal captain Frank Mclintock, commentator Jim Rosenthal and the then England Football Manager Bobby Robson, were present to boost the bidding. It raised £700, an amazing amount of money!

A short time later, Alan Parry and I met at a local Rumbelows store with the lady who had had her savings stolen. The store supplied the new washing machine, which was fitted by a local plumber free of charge. There was sufficient money left to present her with a cheque and to donate some to local charities. There were times when all the effort was more than worthwhile. Well done to all involved.

This was just one example of the better side of human nature. After the horrors of Hungerford were still vivid in everyone's mind, to be involved in a small way in such a heart-warming event went a long way to restore faith in humanity. That is something which we as police officers don't always see that much of.

I thoroughly enjoyed the time in charge of my own station. Being the 'Sheriff' of Gerrards Cross was a great honour and I learnt a good deal about the politics side of being in charge. In some respects it didn't last long enough. Four months into my time there I had a 'phone call from my previous boss on Support Group, chief inspector, Glyn Lambert. He had been highly influential in my career to date and it turned out that he would be again in the near future. He asked me how it was going at Gerrards Cross and if I was enjoying it. When I told him that I was he said something like, "So I don't suppose you would be interested in coming back onto Support Group as one of the inspectors then?"

ARE YOU KIDDING ME? I remember telling him that that my briefcase could be packed and I would be on the road to headquarters in ten minutes if he was serious. He was serious, but it would take a little longer than ten minutes. That was it then, in February 1988 I went back to the Support Group as inspector for the southern area of the force. I genuinely enjoyed my time at Amersham and Gerrards Cross as an inspector, but it was no contest with the opportunity to return to Support Group as one of only two inspectors in the force.

I returned to Gerrards Cross to complete my final task. I was guest speaker at the annual dinner for the combined Chambers of Commerce of Gerrards Cross, Beaconsfield and Chalfont St Peter, held at The Bellhouse Hotel, Beaconsfield. I had been invited soon after my arrival as the newly installed inspector and had accepted. I thought it would be a good opportunity to meet a cross section of local people. There was also a certain amount of arrogance on my part in agreeing to do it. I was confident that I could do after dinner speaking, even though I had never done it before. When I discovered that I would be moving on I gave them the opportunity to find a new speaker, but it was too late by then. As the evening of my debut at public speaking approached, I realised I had made a mistake in accepting the invitation. Little did I know how big a mistake it was to be.

I borrowed a book, which I found useful, giving tips about public speaking. One suggestion I took on board and is still in place to this day was, do not be tempted to have an alcoholic drink before delivering the talk. How glad was I on the night that I had remembered that one. Come the event, I arrived early and found a quiet corner to go over the notes I had prepared. I was seated at the top table with the three chamber presidents, who made me very welcome and pressed me to have a drink before proceedings started. 'No thank you', I remembered the advice but if they offered me a drink after dinner, just try me then!

The sumptuous three course dinner looked and tasted very good, the little that I ate, that is. I was so nervous that my appetite deserted me. The copious amount of wine flowing was also tempting, but I held my resolve not to partake this side of the talk. Whilst we were enjoying the first course the toastmaster leaned over and whispered in the ear of the senior chamber president. He then asked the other two and myself to listen in, he informed us that the band which had been booked had not turned up and they were attempting to trace them. The suggestion was that each president who was due to talk for five minutes, must pad it out to ten each. He asked if I could extend my agreed twenty minutes to thirty? That would hopefully give them time to locate the band. PANIC! I sorted through my cue cards and scribbled some extra bits here and there, changed one or two things and thought that I could probably just about eke it out for thirty minutes.

We were just about to start on the dessert, when the toastmaster again bent the ear of the senior president who was delighted to tell us that the band had been located; they were on their way and would arrive just a little later than planned. In that case it was back to Plan A, five minutes for each of them and twenty for me. Oh no, out with the cue cards to try to restore them to their original content. By the end of coffee, I was a bag of nerves and trying to think how I could get out of this. Perhaps if I fainted I could get away with it. If only my pager would go off and call me out to a firearms job.

All too soon it was my turn to speak. I was on my feet and away I went. The line I was taking related to the occasionally high level of burglaries in the areas covered by the three Chambers. The first couple of funnies I included went down well and the audience, about two hundred people, were laughing in the right places. The top table was situated about halfway down the huge dining room and the entrance door was to my left. I had not realised but the area for the band was to my right, about as far from the entrance door as could be. I was doing well and was relating a true story about a lady who lived in Gerrards Cross. She had returned home to her large house in the afternoon and saw one man at her open front door, another man on the drive and one of her televisions on the front doorstep. She realised what was happening, yes, her house was being burgled. She immediately drove out again to a friend's house from where she telephoned her husband who worked in London. He told her to stay there and he drove from London to his home and guess what, he realised they had been burgled so he then rang the police!

As I got to the part where she saw the men and the television set, the entrance door to the banqueting hall burst open and a band member came in carrying a drum. He had a face like thunder and had clearly been torn off a strip for being late. He was followed by a man carrying cymbals and then a lady with a microphone and stand. They ignored everyone, weaving their way through the tables and placed the items on the small stage area. I was horrified, I didn't know what to do, I realised that I hadn't said anything while this had been going on. They then retraced their steps back out of the banqueting hall. There was a good deal of laughter from the audience but not generated by me. Now the band had gone and I tried to pick up the story.

As I did so the door burst open again and the first man came in with a saxophone. I had now lost it completely but something, some inner being, took me over and I heard myself say, "And she (the lady on her drive) saw a man come out of the house with a saxophone." Pause for laughter, which was forthcoming. When the second band member appeared with a double base I included that in my commentary too. By now the band members had realised 'we' were proving good entertainment, which was causing a great deal of mirth amongst the audience. All I did was latch onto each instrument that they delivered into the ballroom. As the first band member was leaving the room I said, "Much more?"

He replied, "Just one more trip." So, I relayed that as part of my tale. As they were leaving for the last time they declared, "That's it."

I called out, "Here Bert, I've got another one of these dinners next Wednesday, can you make it the same again?"

He called back, "Yes of course, see you then. Same time?

By then the audience was in hysterics. It took a few moments for them to settle for me to finish my story, so I wrapped it up quickly and sat down to rapturous applause.

I was an absolute wreck. People were moving to the bar, but I felt so weak I just sat for a few minutes to compose myself and fortunately, one of the presidents brought me a much needed drink. When I did move to the bar for one more drink before I left for home, I had many positive complimentary comments and congratulations. The Editor of the local newspaper, who I had met previously, said that the commentary was worthy of David Coleman's finest, praise indeed. One couple asked me if it was actually planned with the band! Another man asked what the function was next Wednesday because he would like to see the performance again. What are these people like? What an absolute disaster, well almost. Never again. That is the last time I ever do public speaking, HA! To this day I get a cold shiver every time I go anywhere near The Bellhouse Hotel in Beaconsfield.

The day started a lot earlier for me when I rejoined Support Group and I went straight in at the deep end with a firearms operation at Windsor. We were contacted by the metropolitan police regarding two shooting incidents in London. A male suspect, wanted in connection with both incidents had been traced to an address in Windsor and we had been asked to arrest him. We made our enquiries, blocked off the street, entered the house divided into separate flats and arrested the man. No problems, no shots fired, no-one injured and a good one to get me back into the swing of such operations.

CHAPTER 15

—

It's Murder

Strong arm of the law

One of the main non-firearms duties of Support Group was to give assistance on murder enquiries in a number of ways: house to house enquiries, road checks, sometimes targeting potential suspects and as previously mentioned, specialised fingertip searches at murder scenes. This was to complement the work of SOCO, who covered a more forensic search. The actual investigation was normally headed by a Detective Superintendent and he or she had a team of experienced detectives to conduct all aspects of the enquiry. We performed various ancillary tasks which dovetailed into the operation and all were designed to achieve the ultimate aim, to identify the offender or offenders. In any murder enquiry as the tragic circumstances unfold, a great degree of sensitivity is required. We could be carrying out a detailed fingertip search or be involved in another task, when close family members of the victim would visit the scene. Regretfully, I have been involved in more murder enquiries than I would have ever imagined. Remember, it was that tragic murder in Amersham all those years before which first started me on the Support Group career path.

House to house enquiries were always a vitally important part of the investigation, especially early on when bits and pieces of information would be forthcoming which could then be passed on to the investigation teams. In some respects, it was thought that any police officer could do the house to house work. Tell the officer what was required, give them a clipboard and a form to fill in and away they went. However, history dictates that it was not quite that simple. Support Group officers had gained a great deal of experience and expertise over many years on numerous different enquiries. The main difference was that specific thought was needed as to the precise questions to ask. What were the parameters? For example, the time frame for the people questioned to account for their movements and the age group of those to be interviewed. Many times, experienced Support Group officers working in their twos with their normal crewmate would report back saying that they were not happy with a certain individual that they had interviewed. This would be raised with the Incident Room for further enquiries and investigation.

In an urban setting during house to house enquires, we were always on the lookout for what neighbours would call the know-all, the busybody or the local gossip. This was the old lady, or sometimes a man, who would sit behind their net curtains for most of the day and maybe night surveying the street. They would know everything, who was doing what with whom and when. The difficulty could be getting them to open up and tell all. Sometimes they would make us a cup of tea and talk about all sorts of things, then gradually move the topic to 'the goings on' and then it would all come out. A lot of what we were told was of little or no value, but sometimes there were invaluable nuggets of information.

In April 1983 we were called to the scene of a murder in a heavily wooded area on the Buckinghamshire/Northamptonshire border and our main task was to conduct a fingertip search. A man was walking his dog in Salcey Forest, north of Newport Pagnell, when the dog went into an almost impenetrable area of the woods and would not come out. The man went into the brambles to fetch his dog and saw a skull.

When we arrived, we cordoned off the whole area, taped it into a grid of one metre squares and commenced a detailed search. We soon found a second skull and a number of bones, this indicated that we were looking for evidence relating to two bodies. We got down to the fingertip search, which was exactly as it sounds; on hands and knees in a line very close to your colleague, scraping away and then digging into the surface of the ground. The soil was removed by other members of the team, riddled and examined twice. It soon became obvious that there had been at least one leaf fall since the bodies were left here, indicating that they had been in place for at least twelve months. While the fingertip search was taking place, other colleagues were clearing away a wider area and taping it off. When we had finished the search, which took about ten days, the area had been completely cleared and could have been opened as a picnic area without any further work!

We found sufficient bones and teeth to prove that we had one male and one female victim. We even found a very small bone, the hyoid, which is the only bone in the throat and if fractured it indicates strangulation. We found the hyoid of the female and it was broken. From the teeth we uncovered, the man was identified, a young male from Northampton. This led to the name of his girlfriend and enquiries revealed that neither of them had been seen for some months. She was nineteen years of age and he was twenty-three.

The investigation exposed their connection to a self-styled leader of a gang known as Lucifer's Outlaws. The leader of the gang and his number two were arrested and very quickly confessed to the double murder. They had lured the couple to Salcey Forest, where they been handcuffed to a tree. The girl was forced to watch whilst her fiancé was stabbed ten times and then she was strangled. The two offenders were both later convicted of murder.

There are marked differences between the responsibilities of a constable, sergeant or inspector. This is particularly so on murder investigations. The constable is part of the team, given detailed directions and parameters to work within, whether a fingertip search, other type of search or house to house enquiries. They are supervised by their sergeant. The sergeant also searches but retains an overview of the work being done and co-ordinates his team. An inspector has an even wider view with up to four Support Group teams. It is the inspector's role to oversee all of that and keep in touch with the Incident Room and the Senior Investigating Officer, normally a Detective Superintendent, who must be kept up to date with any changes in the investigation.

Shortly before I left Support Group as a sergeant to be promoted to Inspector at Amersham, during April and May 1987, we were engaged in three murder enquiries, one after the other, which stretched everyone physically and mentally.

In April 1987, I was acting inspector with Support Group. One of the Support Group inspectors was away for some weeks, so I was taking his place for a temporary period until he returned. I was asked to attend a pig farm at Holyport, near Maidenhead, and meet with a Detective Superintendent who was heading a murder enquiry. A twenty-five-year-old woman had been missing for some time and her boyfriend had confessed to her murder. He had shown the detectives the pig farm and said that he had dumped the body there because he knew that the pigs would eat anything.

Our task was simple, search the area where one hundred pigs and piglets were living and see if we could find the body or any trace of it. I met with one of my sergeant colleagues from Support Group and we surveyed the pig slurry and tried to work out our strategy for the search. As we were doing so we were approached by several pigs, one of which had something in its mouth. This turned out to be a human leg bone. We knew then that we would be searching for bones not a body. It was obvious that this was going to be a most unpleasant task.

Two parties of Support Group were engaged for a week working, at best ankle deep and at worst knee deep, in pig slurry and mud. The pigs had apparently lived here quite happily for a number of years and it showed.

The officers engaged on the search did a remarkable job finding several bones and pieces of clothing, some of which showed signs of being burnt. It transpired that the body had been set alight before being dumped. Some small pieces of clothing were identified as belonging to the victim of this awful crime. To find such small items in these conditions and being up to eighteen inches deep in slurry was a magnificent effort.

Four days after we had completed the search at the pig farm we were called to the scene of another murder. Most of those intervening days had been taken as relaxation, recharging the batteries and cleaning all the equipment. This new investigation was most bizarre. A young woman had been found dead, bound, gagged and floating face down in the lake at Taplow, near Maidenhead. Her arms and legs were tied, and her hands were behind her back. A Murder Incident Room was set up, but at that early stage the possibility of suicide could not be ruled out.

Her car was found unlocked about half a mile away in a layby and the lake was not far from where she was living. She was fully clothed when found and had not been sexually assaulted. There were no signs that she had been involved in a struggle. She had died from drowning. She appeared to have everything in her favour; friends said that she was a lovely girl and it seemed most unlikely that she would have committed suicide. It grabbed the imagination of the press who really took it on with massive publicity, front page of the national press: The Lady in The Lake Murder.

Our task was to undertake a detailed search of the immediate surrounds of the lake and out to a car park close to the area. After a couple of days everyone was convinced that she had been murdered. This was confirmed by a 'knots expert', who had examined the rope and other items used to tie her and stated that she could not have tied herself in the way in which she was found. There were several theories put forward, not least by the press. We heard about a kidnap plot that had gone wrong, whereby a gang may have abducted her to gain a share of her family's fortune. There was no evidence whatsoever of that or any of the other spurious claims. It was another example of a tragedy that can strike anywhere at any time.

There had been a major improvement in technology which was used in our part of the operation. The lake was in a rural area and so we took advantage to keep in touch by use of the latest gadget, a mobile phone. Remember this was 1987, and mobile phones were in their infancy. At the start of our involvement in the murder enquiry, I was given a mobile phone so that I could report direct to the Incident Room, as well my boss at HQ. Such was the interest in this case that anything significant found by us needed instant reporting. The only problem was the phone itself, it was huge. It was attached to a battery which resembled a car battery in both size and weight. So much so that as we deployed round the lake to commence the search I had one of my officers carry it for me, well come on, I was an inspector or acting inspector. I couldn't be expected to carry it myself! As perhaps can be imagined, I took a good deal of stick over the carrying of and the use of the thing.

I had been using the phone to contact HQ to update them. Just as I finished a call, a contingent of the press were allowed in alongside the lake to photograph us doing the search. They were intrigued by the latest technology and asked if I would use the mobile phone again so that they could take photos of me doing so. As there was no one else to call at that time, they asked me to pose with the phone as if I was calling someone, which of course I did. I never missed an opportunity to pose for a photo, given the chance. Suffice it to say, there was more stick forthcoming from my lot whilst I was being photographed.

TVP had a very good record in solving major crimes especially murders. However on some occasions the crime was unsolved. This was one such case. Despite raising a massive amount of enquiries which were undertaken by the experienced detectives who worked tirelessly over a period of many weeks, the offender was never found. The case remained open and ten years later further enquiries were made. The circumstances of the murder were similar to several crimes which had occurred in the Midlands and the North of England. Enquiries and comparisons were made in an effort to see if the similarities could throw any light on our murder. Unfortunately nothing substantial was found which took it any further. To date the case remains undetected and is still on TVP's books as unresolved.

Whilst working on a tragic case and fulfilling particularly difficult tasks, there had to be light hearted moments of release, otherwise it could become depressing for those involved. For some people on the outside looking in, it may have seemed heartless for officers involved in such a grim task to be seen laughing when they were on a break. It was the release we all needed to keep sane.

In May 1987, we were looking forward to returning to normality and preparing for more regular duties. I was called out to meet my boss and survey the location for a detailed search in High Wycombe at the scene of another murder. As previously mentioned, and unsurprisingly, the most difficult murder enquiries for everyone are those involving children and this was a case in point. The body of a twelve-year-old boy had been found in a shallow grave, after his parents had reported him missing the previous evening.

He had been subjected to a frenzied attack and found half buried in an isolated wooded area. A man walking his dog came across this when the dog discovered the body partially hidden in undergrowth.

We surveyed the potential search area from the police helicopter which showed it to be vast. There was a pond and a river nearby and the area was known locally as The Black Lagoon. In the initial briefing it was particularly harrowing hearing about the circumstances, especially so for those of us with children of a similar age as the victim. I made sure the search was under way and we were also tasked with vital house to house enquiries. At that early stage of the enquiry there was nothing much to work on, no apparent motive, no suspects, no witnesses and no evidence. That was where the skill of the detectives and the incident room team all pulled together, to try to build a picture of what had gone on in the area and who might have seen anything. People have often been near to an incident such as this, may have seen something or someone and not realised the significance. All the little snippets of information once put together, form a bigger picture. Thus, we would have a starting point.

Anacapa was an example of a system which helped build the picture. It was a Graphical Information Analysing System in the form of a chart. It put together information about a number of people who knew each other or who had met each other, or people who had been seen by witnesses. It used circles and lines to connect them. Each person was circled, and the lines connected them where appropriate. This case was a classic example of the system.

We discovered very early on that the area was used by people walking their dogs. We found an elderly man who wore a hat, scarf and glasses and walked a small terrier dog. A woman wearing a green coat walking a golden Labrador dog was found. A young blonde girl, teenager to twenty years of age, used the area as a short cut on a regular basis. She mentioned the man with the terrier and the woman in the green coat. The woman in the green coat remembered seeing the girl and the man with the terrier dog. They were put onto the Anacapa chart and connected, it was then shown that they had been traced and cleared of any involvement Two of the three people mentioned above also saw a man in his early twenties, white male, 'hanging about and looking uncomfortable' was how he was described. When he was put onto the chart it was plainly obvious that he had not been traced and that therefore became a priority. It just so happened that in this case he was the offender, he was traced and later charged with the murder.

Anacapa was developed in USA after the assassination of President J F Kennedy in Dallas, Texas in 1963. It was named after an island off California on the west coast of America, which is perpetually shrouded in mist. When the mist rises it all becomes clear, hence Anacapa means, 'the parting of the mist'. Aptly named for its use in major incidents as shown by this classic example here. Nowadays of course it is all computerised, but a glance at that chart on the wall showed us immediately the current situation regarding who was still to be traced and interviewed.

CHAPTER 16

—

More Murder Mysteries

"A scrimmage near the line"

One advantage of being a Support Group officer was that our place of duty was the whole of the TVP area, so we found ourselves working at many different places. I rarely worked in my local town, however in February 1989, there was a murder enquiry which caused me to work closer to home than normal.

A mother of two young children had been found brutally stabbed and battered to death in her home in St Leonards, a village near Chesham. She had failed to collect the children from school that afternoon. When her husband was alerted, he telephoned a neighbour who went to the house, saw through the window that something was wrong and contacted the police. They broke in and found the body of the young mother. There was no sexual assault; it looked like a burglary which had possibly gone wrong. Her car, a Ford Fiesta, had been taken and was found abandoned in the old part of Chesham, some six miles away. About three hundred yards from her house a mountain bike was found. It had apparently been stolen from the Pond Park area of Chesham.

We started with several tasks; a search in the immediate area of the scene of the murder and the surrounds of the house and another search moving out from where the car had been abandoned. In addition, we commenced house to house enquiries in the village. This was especially important for two reasons: Firstly, to find out whether anyone had any useful information or seen anything which could be helpful. Secondly, it was very important to have a high-profile police presence to reassure the local people. There were two hundred people living in the village and they were numb with shock that such an awful crime had taken place where, in their words, 'nothing ever happened'. The victim was known in the village and was well liked, just part of a normal loving family. We also carried out house to house enquiries in the area from where the mountain bike had been stolen. It was from these enquiries that a breakthrough came.

At the end of each day there was a de-briefing of both teams, search and house to house, to highlight anything which required further investigation. One of the house to house teams had interviewed a young man who lived close to the place where the bike had been stolen. He had seemed very uncomfortable, vague and evasive to the officers, but eventually gave a hazy indication of where he was supposed to have been when the murder had taken place. Both officers agreed when they left the house that they 'didn't like him'. That was nothing personal, it just meant that they were not happy with his answers, they felt he was holding something back or even telling a pack of lies. That did not necessarily mean anything untoward; there are people who do not like the police. Perhaps they had been in trouble with the police in the past and so, for whatever reason, we sometimes faced negativity when confronting people in their own home or on the street. This suspicion was highlighted to the incident room for further enquiries and checks to be made.

As a result, the officers were asked to return to the house and question the young man again in a little more detail and to further check his movements at the relevant times. It was sometimes a good tactic; having the same officers return and ask further questions to see if they got the same feeling and same answers to their questions. His version of events at the time of the murder didn't check out. He was not where he said he had been and he therefore came into the frame as a possible suspect. Further in-depth enquiries were made into his movements and his supposed alibi and as a result shortly after, one of the detective teams called at his house and arrested him on suspicion of murder. He was interviewed and later charged with the offence. In January the following year he was convicted of this dreadful and unnecessary crime which had left a lovely family totally devastated.

It's May 1989 and another murder, this time at Oxford and the victim was a reclusive ninety-four-year-old lady living alone. Apparently, she only used the ground floor of her rambling three storey, but ramshackle manor house on the outskirts of Oxford. She was discovered by neighbours who called the police when they noticed the milk and papers, which were normally delivered through an open window, had not been taken in. There were signs of disturbance with everything turned upside down as if the offender(s) had been searching for the money, which local rumour had it, she was hoarding at the house. It transpired that she had been strangled.

We were briefed as to our early involvement. Our initial role was to conduct an outside search including the overgrown garden and outhouse. Once SOCO had finished their work inside the house, we would take over and conduct a detailed search sorting every item of property. At the same time another team would start the house to house enquiries on the nearby estate, in an effort to generate a picture of the comings and goings of people in the vicinity of the property.

The first three days proved extremely fruitful in all areas. The search of the inside of the premises revealed a number of things which proved useful to the enquiry. The house to house teams had come forward with a basketful of helpful information relating to several people, some of whom were of interest and required looking at in greater detail. The detectives from the incident room were also pulling out all the stops in the different lines of enquiry, which were building rapidly. By day five a pattern was starting to emerge on the house to house enquiries. Many of the local residents were saying things like, "Well you know who it is, everyone knows, so why haven't you arrested him yet?" Despite trying to persuade them, no one would name who they thought was responsible.

Another couple of days and the suspect was indeed arrested and later charged with murder. That was seven days of long hours, everyone working very hard together to solve yet another murder. This time, of a frail old lady living out her last days, a harm to no one.

It was the next month, June 1989, and onto another murder, this time in Slough. The body of a murdered man was discovered in Salt Hill Park in the early hours of the morning. He had been strangled. Two men discovered the body behind the public toilets in the park. The area was renowned as a meeting place for homosexuals, so an added element to this murder enquiry was the need to seek help and co-operation from the gay community. It appeared at the outset as if robbery was the intention because some items had been taken from the victim. There had been a series of muggings of homosexuals in this area, some reported, some not.

The fingertip search at the scene and surrounding area was very detailed and not the most pleasant of tasks, but vitally important as always. The house to house enquiries also included stopping and questioning people in the park to ascertain their reason for being there. This was as crucial as ever but required a good degree of sensitivity when broaching the subject of their sexuality. It gleaned some interesting answers. It also highlighted a number of men who frequently used the park to meet other like-minded men. Eventually information was forthcoming about men being attacked and mugged and some descriptions became available. As with other murder enquiries we quickly built a picture of events which moved the enquiry forward.

Two days into this enquiry we received requests to assist with other operations in our police force area. There had been a stabbing at Wokingham, an armed robbery in Banbury, another armed robbery in Hungerford, a serious assault at Milton Keynes and a report of Animal Rights activists preparing incendiary devices to be placed in branches of McDonalds. There was also a robbery on Friday night and another one on Saturday night elsewhere in Slough. We needed to see if there was any connection with the murder and the muggings. Apart from that nothing much was happening! We eked out our resources as best we could and continued to progress with the murder enquiry. There had been some good finds on the search and, coupled with information gained from the house to house enquiries and the good work of the detectives, a small number of people were highlighted who may have been involved, so we made a number of arrests.

Five days into this enquiry our searches were completed, and we had almost finalised the house to house enquiries. We therefore left a small team to tidy it all up and moved on to other commitments. As we left it was looking very positive that the offender would be identified. Sure enough, the process had worked and he was eventually found and charged with the murder.

The day after winding up at Slough, we were called to another child death this time at High Wycombe. Two schoolgirls, fifteen and thirteen years of age, were walking through an area of woodland when they discovered the body of a new born baby. They carried the tiny corpse to a children's home about a mile away where the staff called the police. The girls, who were clearly horrified by what they had discovered, were able to show us exactly where they found the body in an isolated part of the wood. This was very important because the baby had been hidden, so was presumably dead when it was left. If it had still been alive, it would more likely have been left somewhere out in the open, where it could have been seen easily. A priority under such circumstances is to find the mother with a great deal of urgency. It was likely that she would require medical attention and would need to be found quickly. It was thought at that early stage that the baby had been less than twenty-four hours old.

In an enquiry such as this we were desperate for a starting point. What had we got? An isolated wood, no houses nearby, no apparent witnesses and we were attempting to trace a woman, or girl who had been pregnant twenty-four hours before, but was no longer. It would be likely that she would know the neighbourhood because of the isolated area of woodland, therefore she was probably local. With no immediate house to house enquiries to be done, we got on with the search at the scene. It looked early on as if the birth had not taken place there, it was just that the baby had been dumped there. Not much to go then. There was a huge area nearby which was used as a rubbish tip, this certainly did not help the searchers. A ripped carrier bag was found with what appeared to be blood inside. It may not have been connected with so much rubbish and animal activity, but we hoped that it was.

We started on a Wednesday and by Saturday we had identified and traced twenty-five females who had been pregnant and had given birth very recently. Various enquiries had also highlighted several useful leads. One good example was that the day before the girls had found the baby, a woman had seen a car at the edge of the woods near a pathway leading directly to where the baby had been discovered. The witness said that with the car were a man and a young woman, who was very distressed. They may of course have been totally unconnected with the dead baby. If that was the case, we still needed to trace them because they were two more potential witnesses who may have had vital information. We completed our responsibilities fairly quickly and pulled out, leaving it to the experienced detectives who do the job best.

To all intents and purpose we had finished and done all we could in this tragic case. However, we kept in contact as to it's progress. It was always very sad to hear that despite everyone's best efforts no satisfactory outcome was forthcoming.

It was 7.00am on a Sunday morning in July 1989 when a group of holidaymakers boating on the River Thames, near Windsor Castle, came across the body of a male floating in the river. It was a man from Slough and he had multiple stab wounds in the head and chest. He had been reported missing that morning by his wife after he had left their house at 2.30am and failed to return. His car was found about four miles away. Initial thoughts were that he had been killed elsewhere, then driven to the river near where he was found and presumably thrown in.

In the water near the body was a large piece of curtain like material and a plastic sheet. These items may have been used to wrap and transport the body to where it was dumped. This was all speculation, but it gave a possible starting point which the incident commander, the Detective Superintendent, was looking for. There was not much of a search for us to do, so we started with the house to house enquiries at three separate locations: alongside the river where the body was discovered, where the victim's car was found and the area surrounding his home address.

Examination of the car showed some blood on the nearside door and some brown curtain like material, similar to that found in the river near the body. There was some great work by the detectives in the couple of days following the discovery of the body. On interviewing the victim's wife, it transpired that she knew that the body of her husband had been found wrapped in a brown curtain because it had been reported as such in The Sun newspaper. On examination of the house it was noted there were no curtains at one of the bedroom windows. A detailed search of the inside of the house showed a photo of the lounge taken some time previously when there were brown curtains hanging at the lounge window. What a coincidence! The breakthrough came from those observations.

Three days into the enquiry and an associate, a friend of the victim's wife had been traced and interviewed. He confessed to his involvement in the murder and to transporting the body to the river wrapped in the bedroom curtain. There were five of them involved altogether including some family members, his wife being one of them, all were arrested and charged with being concerned together in the murder.

In February 1990, we were called to the scene of a murder on the Britwell Estate in Slough. A well-known local man who had just been released from prison, was found lying dead in the hallway of his home at 1.00am having been shot in the head from close range with a shotgun. It appears that he had answered the door and was met with a shotgun blast. Enquiries revealed that the dead man had received death threats some time previously and slogans such as, 'Joe you're dead', had been daubed on walls in Slough. Engaging local people in house to house enquiries can be extremely difficult in some situations and this was a classic example. A lot of people did not want to talk to the police whether they knew anything or not. That was quite understandable, when such a violent act had taken place close to where they and their family lived. We did discover that there was talk of, 'blokes from London', who were after him and had apparently found him.

Eight days after the murder in Slough, we were dispatched to Beaconsfield, not very far away, to another murder which was totally different in every way. In a small quiet cul-de-sac, a teenaged schoolboy and his parents were found savagely bludgeoned to death in their home. Local people reported seeing a man in the back garden of the family home; he said something to some schoolchildren and then headed for a small copse of trees nearby, put a rope noose around his neck and climbed a tree. When the house was checked, the parents were both found dead and their fifteen year old son's body was found in the garden shed. All three had been beaten and stabbed a number of times. The man in the tree was clearly the offender and with the noose still around his neck he threatened to jump and kill himself.

It generated a tremendous amount of publicity with a circus of national press in the area. I was aware that once the horrific nature of the murders became known, a lot of people would think, and did say, 'Let him jump, it's what he deserves' or something similar. Unfortunately, it was not that simple, and a dialogue was started with the offender. Eventually, he was persuaded to remove the noose from his neck and to climb down where he was arrested for the murders. It had been discovered by then that he had got into drugs some two years previously. He had also been a mental patient at a local hospital a short time before this tragedy. He had formed a friendship with the son of the family and that was the connection between him and them. It appeared that he had fallen out with the young lad and that was thought to be the trigger for those awful crimes.

In April 1991, we became involved in one of those enquiries which really grabbed the imagination of everyone including the national press, who went overboard in its coverage. We were asked to assist in what was originally a missing person enquiry. Most observers and those involved in the case, including the investigating teams, were convinced almost from the outset that it was a murder enquiry.

An Oxford University student, Rachel Mclean, had vanished days before her examinations after kissing her boyfriend goodbye at Oxford railway station.

The nineteen-year-old young woman from Blackpool was living in a Victorian terraced house in Cowley, Oxford. She shared her lodgings with four other female students. She was a second-year student studying at St Hilda's College, Oxford. All enquiries revealed that she was a sensible girl and very well thought of by all who knew her. She had disappeared from the face of the earth with no explanation, no clothes were missing and her bank account had not been touched. Her boyfriend, a student studying at Nottingham University and originally from New Zealand, had given a detailed description of how she saw him off on the train at the station and he had not seen or heard from her since. Her four flatmates could throw no light on the situation as she had never done anything like this before.

We assisted by fulfilling our usual dual roles; a search at the house where she lived and house to house enquiries in the vicinity of the property and at the railway station where she was last seen by her boyfriend. It is correct to say that, unusually for us, we found absolutely nothing to help with the enquiry. Remembering that it was still a missing person enquiry, there were limitations as to how it could be conducted. Questions were constantly being asked of the investigating officer such as, whether or not it should be a murder enquiry. We continued our work and moved our search out to nearby parks and open areas and still found nothing. It was a very frustrating time for all involved, but one could only imagine the dreadful experience that Rachel's parents were going through. In our own private world when we discussed the case, based on our previous experience, we were absolutely convinced that it would only end one way.

After eighteen days of the enquiry it was still continuing in the same direction. I was contacted by my boss, I was by now an inspector on Support Group overseeing the searching and the house to house enquiries. I was asked to meet with him and the investigating officer. It was time for a change of direction and we were asked to conduct a detailed search of the whole of the house, in effect to tear it apart if necessary, to ensure that Rachel was not there.

It was mid-afternoon and I tasked one party of officers to complete their current enquiries as soon as possible and meet at the house to conduct a search in the manner described. One of our officers, who was very experienced in searches such as this, was the first to arrive at the house. As he was waiting for his colleagues to arrive he chatted to a couple of Rachel's flatmates and asked about certain areas which were now going to be searched. He was on the ground floor looking into a corner of a room whilst making preparations as to how the search would be carried out. He moved a piece of wood which he then realised formed part of the wall. When he moved it, he could see that there was access to an area under the house, an open area. There were lots of pillars of bricks visible on which the house was standing. All the while one of the girls from the flat was behind him still chatting away. As he looked further under the house and around a corner to his right, almost looking back on himself, he could see a carpet with what appeared to be something large rolled up inside. He knew exactly what it was, he had found Rachel.

I can only praise the professionalism of this officer, trying to imagine what was going through his mind at that moment was difficult, but he dealt with the situation magnificently.

He backed out of where he was and, in his words, tried to sound normal and not give any clue as to what he had just seen. He asked the young woman if she would mind making him a cup of tea before the others arrived, or they would all want one, and off she went. He then closed the access to the area under the house, went out to his police vehicle and called me on the radio. All he asked was would I meet him at the property, nothing more just that. It was strange, but as I made my way to meet him, I remember thinking, 'He's found her', I can't explain why, it was just something in his voice. I arrived about ten minutes later and there were a number of Support Group already there. They were hanging about outside the house and included, surprisingly, some who were not supposed to be there. They said that they had heard the radio message as well and had thought the same as me. Of course, they were right, Rachel's body was rolled up inside the carpet.

Shortly after, the boyfriend was arrested, interviewed and two days later charged. He was later convicted of Rachel's murder and sentenced to life imprisonment. As I write this, twenty-two years later, I am aware that this man was released from prison some time ago having served his sentence, but Rachel is still dead and her parents will never get over the loss of a treasured daughter.

After the body was discovered, there was some implied criticism and questions as to why had it taken the police eighteen days to find the body. There was the difficulty from the outset of the difference between what was initially a missing person enquiry or a murder enquiry. There was no evidence to suggest that she had come to any harm, other than a 'copper's intuition'. With a missing person enquiry the house is not torn apart; the search is for the person not a body. Aside from all that, what a brilliant job was done by Woody, the officer who found the body.

Three weeks after we had finished at Oxford and had got that one out of our system, we were sent to Slough where a headless body had been found in a school driveway.

At 7.20am on a May morning in 1991 a caretaker approaching the school where he worked, saw a heavily bloodstained bedspread lying in the gutter just yards from the primary school. As he got closer he saw that it was wrapped around a headless body. Less than an hour later and approximately half a mile away, the head was found in a black plastic bin bag. We were called to the scene whilst the detectives began their enquiries into the murder. All our equipment arrived from police headquarters and we then put up screens to protect the two crime scenes. It also prevented the public, especially the children attending the primary school, from viewing the grisly sights. With the screens in place we were able to start our fingertip search in an effort to look for clues. Once that had been completed, and by now the victim had been identified as a local man living in Slough, we transferred to his home address to search. We also set up the house to house enquiries at the places the body and head were found and in close proximity to his home.

The enquiries proved very difficult, the victim was an Asian man with many relatives and friends in the area. It was a difficult line to tread to elicit information, when they were all still grieving over their loss.

Eventually, a picture started to emerge and soon after several potential offenders were highlighted, mainly local people. We were eventually given the go ahead to conduct a search at a house and garden, as well as a car suspected of featuring in the commission of the murder. Early on in this search some items we found may have had particular relevance to the murder.

The detailed nature of the search included the remains of a bonfire in the rear garden and the shed. In the house we searched the inside of the water tank in the loft, the loft roof spaces, behind the bath, the ceiling in the bedroom, up the chimney, the u bends and the outside drains. On searching and examining the car, a spot of blood and a bloodied footprint were found. Together with other items discovered in various places a case was starting to build. A short time later some arrests were made and eventually the account of what had happened was revealed and a number of people were charged with the murder.

In August the following year two men were convicted of the murder at the Old Bailey and jailed for life. Council for the prosecution admitted the murder appeared to be motiveless. There was a suggestion that the victim was having an affair with a relative of the offenders but any evidence of that was inadmissible at court. A further suggestion was put forward that the motive related to money owed to the victim but that could not be proven so the murder remained motiveless. The murder weapon was never found but it was believed to have been a sword.

Another successful operation completed. Due in no small way to the excellent cooperation between the experienced detectives, with their areas of expertise, and us, the uniformed specialists performing our role all working together superbly well. It was a classic example of an extremely difficult investigation but ended with the right result.

CHAPTER 17

–

Firearms Operations

Stop, Thief!

A s mentioned previously the primary function of Support Group was to provide a firearms response for TVP. When I first joined and was authorised as a firearms officer, that included all aspects of firearms operations. We provided armed support to the close protection officers for royalty and VIPs. We supported the armed officers required at static locations such as Chequers, the Prime Minister's country retreat, as previously mentioned. We provided a Tactical Firearms Team and were called in to resolve any firearms incidents. We also provided the armed team used when information and intelligence was received that an armed robbery or armed incident was going to take place. Later on, was the advent of Armed Response Vehicles (ARVs), these too were manned by Support Group officers.

The principle of having armed officers in the public arena was, and still is, a very serious matter. Whenever the authorisation for the issue of firearms to officers was considered, it was always given the greatest thought before such a decision was made. In any firearms operation an officer of the rank of Assistant Chief Constable (ACC) or above must have given the authorisation for officers to be armed. Therefore, to make that decision, he or she must have been in possession of all the information available, consideration would be given to all other alternatives before firearms were issued. In urgent cases where there was insufficient time to go through that process, officers of a lower rank could authorise arming, but these were still senior officers. In extremely urgent situations officers crewing the ARVs are permitted to arm themselves but must notify the police headquarters as soon as practicable.

To assist in the process of whether there was sufficient information and intelligence for firearms to be authorised, the ACC, as above, will always have the benefit of advice from a Firearms Tactical Advisor. There were a small number of them within TVP and they were normally the two inspectors and the chief inspector of the Support Group. At various times there were other experienced officers who could perform that task. I fulfilled that role when I rejoined the Support Group as an inspector.

The responsibility of the tactical advisor was to explain to the ACC the options available if firearms were to be issued and how the operation would be implemented and the likely success or otherwise. It would also cover the possible consequences if firearms were not issued and something would need to be done, but without firearms cover. There were instances when the information was not strong enough and more work needed to be done on the background and the intelligence before consideration would be given to authorise the issue of firearms. In every case where firearms authorisation was sought, the whole process would be fully documented and the reasons for the decisions made.

When dealing with armed offenders, either in a pre planned operation or attempting arrests after the crime has been committed, there are a number of tactical options available. However, the overriding priority under any such circumstances is always safety. It starts with the safety of the public, the police officers involved and the safety of the offenders as well. It was always the aim to resolve the situation with no shots fired, no one injured, and any offenders arrested.

Whenever faced with an armed operation a number of options were always considered and the one with the best chance of achieving the aim was chosen. There was never a 'one-size-fits-all' preference. One of the options always considered, was to do nothing. It may be that the information on offer wasn't good enough to warrant an armed response. Alternatively, it may have been too difficult to carry out a safe operation, but I must comment that whilst 'doing nothing' was a consideration, there was usually something which could be done. Operations to arrest armed offenders in the early days, saw the use of armed raids of premises where they were believed to be (the running raid). Normally that was their home address but could be elsewhere. This was the most popular choice for several reasons. When carried out correctly it was usually resolved quickly. Not only that, it was very exciting crashing someone's front door in at 4.00am. Charging into a house and arresting the offender whilst they were still in possession of the gun was always the best evidence to present to a court. It also meant that a criminal firearm was removed from circulation.

The fact that this was the one we liked doing best didn't cloud our judgement as to what was the best option to utilise. Each and every time all options were considered on their merits, the best one chosen was the one most likely to achieve our aim.

Regrettably, some years later there were two incidents, one in London and one in Birmingham, where tragedies occurred on running raids and innocent people were shot and killed. After that we erred on the side of caution even when the running raid appeared to be the best option. That meant that we were required to come up with other alternatives.

If the chosen option was to contain the premises and call the offender out it could entail closing roads and evacuating people from nearby houses. The outcome of this tactic was never certain of course, and it may have taken hours or even days to conclude.

A call out, as mentioned above, was considered a safer option but had the potential to cause problems for anyone else in the premises who could become a hostage. This operation required an armed containment of the property to ensure that the offender(s) couldn't escape from the building. It may also have required evacuating anyone in close proximity to the target premises safely and quietly. Once everything was in place, contact would be made with anyone inside the premises and attempts made to persuade the suspect to come to the door and follow instructions. In the majority of cases that was exactly what happened. Sometimes it took several attempts to convince the suspects to make the sensible choice. Most times it was resolved fairly quickly. If the target premises were in 'bandit country', an area where we could expect some of the local community to be hostile to police, we would have to saturate the immediate area with armed police and local officers to support us. In those circumstances the last thing we wanted was for an armed siege to go on for days. We were faced with that prospect on one particular firearms operation in an area where we knew there would be a great deal of hostility. We were almost certain that the offender would not do as he was instructed and comply with our intructions. He would be aware that the longer he remained in his house the more likely it was that we would get a lot of grief from the local community. Under those circumstances we could not risk causing a major public disorder disturbance so a running raid was the chosen option. The raid was carried out quickly and worked to perfection. In, offender captured, out and away before anyone else locally was aware of what was happening. Job done.

As equipment improved and we gained more experience with every operation, we were able to modify the callout. Once we had added armoured Land Rovers to our vehicle fleet, as a direct result of the Hungerford shootings of August 1987, we were able to use them to drive right up to buildings and call offenders out from within the Land Rover. In the same way when ballistic shields, similar to riot shields but bullet proof, were available we could open a front door of a house and call out the offender from the safety of the shield. If any of these options were not possible we could always consider the use of subterfuge.

One deception used was when I dressed as a postman from the Royal Mail with a parcel to deliver. On knocking the door, the offender answered, I grabbed him and dragged him out onto the front path. By this time my colleagues had joined me from their secreted place nearby and the man was arrested safely, quickly and quietly. An immediate search of the house found the gun we had been told he was in possession of.

An operation of this type highlights the planning, ingenuity and thought process which goes into searching for an answer to a problem which must be resolved; all 'what ifs' must be considered. Hopefully we highlighted them all during the planning and briefing. It's only at this point when the crucial part of the operation commences, in this case purporting to be the postman, that those 'what ifs' resurface in my mind. Having been given the 'Go', my hand is on the garden gate and I am walking up the path to the front door. What if his mate has seen us preparing and moving into place and phoned him to warn him? What if he is waiting behind that door with gun in hand? What if he comes out of the door pointing the gun while I am halfway up the path and he doesn't believe I'm a postman? All those thoughts are crystallised in fractions of a second and dismissed just as quickly. Confidence is gained because of the assurance and certainty that we have got it right, it's a good well considered plan. The backup of colleagues is close by, close enough to touch but still out of sight, and they are the very best there is. Then, before you know it, it's all over and the correct result is achieved. That's another gun wielding criminal off the streets, brilliant.

A number of unmarked, often referred to as 'plain' vans were also added to our fleet and we were able to use them in a number of ways. If arrest at a premise was unfavourable, other methods were available. Sometimes, information was made known that the offender always left his house, perhaps to go to work, using a particular car. This presented an opportunity to put an armed team in a van nearby. At the optimum moment, we would leap out of the van and make the arrest on the street, providing it was safe to do so.

At a time when armed robberies were especially prevalent, we sometimes found ourselves in difficulty when intelligence came in that one was due to take place. In an ideal situation we would 'plot up' close to the premises, e.g. a building society or bank. On occasions, we would be inside the building, either masquerading as a member of staff whilst an armed team secreted themselves inside but out of view of the public. When the baddies arrived at the premises the 'Strike' would be called and the offenders would be arrested on the pavement in possession of their weapons. We would have a back stop inside the premises with armed officers who would deploy to the door in case any offenders attempted to get inside.

When authorisation of the plan was given to resolve such a problem in this way it provided the best opportunity of convicting the offenders. If arrested by armed police on the pavement, in possession of guns and balaclavas etc. and just about to run into a building society or bank, then there was a good chance they would be convicted. The problem was and still is that as previously stated the safety of the public was paramount. To mount an operation outside a building society or bank, which was invariably in the High Street, could put the public at risk. Therefore, for safety reasons a 'pavement job' was not always authorised even though it may have been the favoured option. In some instances, making the arrests whilst the offenders were en-route or even earlier and charging them with Conspiracy to commit Robbery rather than catching them in the act was the chosen option for safety reasons but it made the likelihood of a conviction more difficult to secure.

Once, at Milton Keynes, we were called out from home after a firearms incident had occurred; the local CID officers had identified the offender and where he lived. They had surveillance on his house and were convinced that he was indoors. This was when a raid on the house was considered to be the best option. Everything was in place, the optimum time of about 4.30am was reached, the front door was crashed in and we, as armed officers, ran in and covered all rooms. The offender was still in bed and was arrested with no problems at all. Our debriefing concluded that it was a good job, well planned and executed to perfection.

Some months later we were again called out to Milton Keynes in the middle of the night. On arrival we were informed that the man we had arrested previously had escaped from custody some time before. He had been hiding out but was now believed to be at the address where we had arrested him on the first occasion. The potential problem was that he knew what our procedures were, he knew what we did and how we did it and could possibly have taken steps to prevent us doing it again.

After considering different options, we again came back to the raid as the best choice, backing our judgement that we were better than him and could do it once more. At the optimum time we crashed the door, I was designated with my crewmate to take the main bedroom. As we ran into the room he was half out of bed reaching for a handgun on the bedside table. Once we pointed out that it was a bad idea and he might like to reconsider, he lay face down and allowed himself to be arrested for a second time. At the subsequent debrief we considered what we would do if we were called out to do him again, not sure of the answer, but fortunately it never happened. The hydraulic door opener we first used at the Grendon Underwood prison siege would have been great in this situation.

Once we had such a door opener ourselves, it was used to great effect many times when raiding premises. I was part of the raid team when we first used it and it was so effective and quiet in popping the front door, that we crept into the house, into the bedroom of the offender and had to wake him up to arrest him!

Despite the serious nature of firearms operations, as with most police work, there are moments of humour which lighten the mood. We were called out one night to a location in Berkshire where an incident of road rage had taken place. In the resultant confrontation, one of the men involved threatened the other person with a handgun.

The victim reported to the police and gave the registration number of the offender's car. He didn't live in our area, but the local police went to his address and his wife informed them that he was currently attending a residential course at a college not too far from where the incident had occurred. We were able to call out the Bursar, who confirmed the address that the man was staying at was in a three storey residential block within the college grounds.

We contained the whole block and placed the armoured Land Rover at the front of the building. Our target room was on the ground floor and was in the middle of twelve doors, all fairly close together. We had decided on a call out from the armoured Land Rover and we used the public-address loudspeaker on the vehicle. Very clear and loud instructions were given and repeated three times along the lines of: "(Named person) you in the building, you are surrounded by armed police. Come to the front door with your hands in the air and follow my instructions."

After a short time, the door opened, a man appeared in the doorway with his hands up; he was told to step out onto the pathway. At that point, three doors down, five doors down and two doors away in the other direction, the doors opened and a man stepped out from each doorway with hands in the air. They were all told to stand still whilst we dealt with our offender, who did exactly as he was told and was arrested. A search of his room revealed an imitation but very realistic blank firing self-loading pistol. Once we were secure we spoke to the others who had come out of their rooms and discovered that two out of the three had been in their room with a young lady whom they had met on their course and were staying the night! What the third man owned up to, who could tell? Clearly guilty consciences all round. In fact, one of them was convinced that his wife had discovered his dirty little secret and she had sent us to get him. Nice idea.

Another funny thing happened on a firearms call out from home when I was sergeant on Support Group. Previously, one of my officers had announced at work that he and his wife were now in possession of the latest bit of technology, an answer phone! It was new and none of us had one except Chris. He explained that it was his wife's and she needed it for her work. A few days later came the phone call to me in the middle of the night, to turn the team out to a firearms incident at Milton Keynes. I rang my officers one by one, always an interesting event. They usually answered quickly.

One of them only ever picked up the phone having been woken from his slumbers but never said anything. I always gave him the information, what it was, where we were going to meet and then I had him repeat it back to me to make sure he had got it.

On this call out, Chris was the last one to be rung as he lived the closest to where we were meeting. After three rings this very friendly female voice came on the line and said, "Hi, we cannot take your call at the moment, please leave a message and we will get back to you." What the hell was going on? It was 3 o'clock in the morning and even if it is a new toy, who the hell has their answer phone on at that time of night? So, I left a very short, sharp message for my man giving the details of the call out. I then made my way to Milton Keynes and, on arrival, gathered all the information as to the current situation. I then went to find my team to brief them and they were all there, including Chris of answer phone fame. He was smiling throughout and whilst we were getting our equipment on I asked him about the smile. He told me that he had just had the weirdest experience. When he and his wife went to bed that evening, for some strange reason they placed the answer phone in the wardrobe. I was going to ask why but thought better of it. However, he continued. He awoke at 3.00am to hear his sergeant, me, who appeared to be in the wardrobe shouting, "I don't care if you have got a bloody answer phone. When I ring to call you out I need to speak to you so get your ******* arse to Milton Keynes and meet me there. It's urgent, a gun job." Yes, he was right, it must have been weird. I was still wondering about the answer phone in the wardrobe, best not to ask.

A shooting was reported near Reading, where a man had advertised a boat for sale. When a potential buyer turned up he shot the seller with a handgun, left him for dead and stole the launch which was moored on the River Thames. The TVP marine section was alerted and tasked with finding the stolen boat. Sergeant Denton and PC Joel, the crew of the police launch 'Sit Pax', set off on this difficult task, made even harder as darkness grew.

They did a magnificent job and by about 2.30am had found the boat moored at Harleyford Marina, Marlow. Two parties of Support Group were called out and we met at the marina. The advice from our river patrol colleagues was that it looked like someone was on board. One problem was that it was possible to start the engine and 'drive off' (forgive the lack of nautical terminology) without coming out from the inner part of the boat. Therefore, that person could make off in the boat without ever putting himself 'on offer'.

A running raid was ruled out owing to the very small entrance into the boat, which restricted access. A plan was devised whereby the police launch would stand off in mid-stream. There would be armed officers on board whilst the remainder would deploy around the boat from the land side. We would then attempt to make contact and call out the offender. It was believed that he was still in possession of the handgun used earlier. My colleague Steve Beveridge and I were allocated the position on the police launch with the two marine section officers. Our role was to dissuade the offender from making off in the boat or diving into the river.

Everything was in place and our illustrious leader, the Support Group chief inspector John Poole, was ready to make contact through a loud hailer, so he started. "Ahoy there, you on the boat." AHOY THERE! Where did that come from? Well I was laughing so much I nearly dropped my gun in the Thames. It did however have the desired effect. After a few more calls, a man appeared on our side of the boat clearly looking to get away but seeing armed officers on the police launch he must have thought better of it. We gesticulated to him and he was told to follow instructions from the officers on land. He did so, walked off the boat and gave himself up. He was the offender responsible for the shooting. We recovered the gun and the situation was resolved without further incident. The seller of the boat recovered, and the offender was later charged. It also put a whole new emphasis on what to say when making contact and calling out an offender. I could only imagine if that we had to call an offender from an ice cream van, I might say, "Oy Mr Whippy, can you hear me?"

One potentially difficult operation, started with a briefing with the Regional Crime Squad (RCS) they dealt with major crimes, and clearly required a number of armed officers. The information was that a burglary was due to take place at a large manor house which was occupied by a well-known family. The house stood in acres of grounds and was not in view from public roads. The proceeds of the burglary were apparently intended as funds to support terrorism. One of the offenders was believed to be carrying a gun when the crime was due to take place. A difficulty for us getting to the house was that it was possible that the baddies were already watching it and may have been secreted within the grounds.

At the briefing we were given quite specific information as to how the burglary would go down. The man who was going to do the breaking in was a professional burglar. It was thought that he was intending to gain entry via a first-floor window, find the main staircase, go down the stairs to the ground floor and make his way into the drawing room where the treasures were kept. He would then choose certain specific items of high value. He would probably leave the house by the same route used to gain entry. It was decided that two parties (teams) of Support Group officers were required to ensure safety for all and to guarantee the arrest of the offenders. One team would be on the ground floor hidden in various places and it was their role to arrest the offenders once they had reached that point. That was the primary role and it went to the Southern Support Group team because the house was in their area. That meant that my team, I was sergeant on the Northern team, had an important role but not at the sharp end. It was our task to secrete ourselves on the first floor at the far end of the corridor leading to the main staircase. Once the offenders went down the stairs we would deploy along the corridor, the landing, to ensure that they had no way out if something went wrong and they tried to escape back up the stairs. We were to be the backstop and back up to our Support Group colleagues on the ground floor.

To get to the house unobserved was an issue, so we were transported in a furniture delivery van and were able to get into the house without being seen even if anyone was watching. On the journey one of the team thought it was a good idea to make a start on his sandwiches. We had Foxy the dog handler with us and his German Shepherd Satan who took great interest in the contents of the sandwich box. The dogs attention to the contents of the box was total with his nose close in giving the sarnies the once over. We all found it highly amusing as did his handler. Not so sure about the owner of the sandwich box, he had less grub than he started with but now he had a new four legged friend.

The family had been moved to a location away from the premises for their own safety. Once inside, we got to our first floor spot along the corridor leading away from the top of the stairs. We found several rooms at the far end and used the last room, a bedroom, as our base and settled down to wait. It was normal for us to wait like this, sometimes for hours and even then, for whatever reason, the operation may or may not happen. We formulated a plan of how we would react and deploy and discussed a number of possible scenarios. We always considered that the unexpected might happen and things may not go exactly to plan. Remember the baddies never came to any of our briefings, so they did not always know what we expected them to do!

Once all my officers were briefed as to their specific roles we relaxed and waited. The bedroom was too crowded, so we took over the bedroom next door as well, then we could relax with some degree of comfort. We were well served on this operation by Crime Squad surveillance officers who were in a range of different places throughout the grounds. Their duty was to remain outside and report in at regular intervals to update us; we would deal with the armed operation inside the house.

Every fifteen minutes or so we would receive a message in our earpieces from the surveillance team declaring, "No change, no change." This meant, nothing happening, no sign of the baddies. During this time we took the opportunity to have our refreshments, sandwiches or similar brought in by each officer. The situation carried on in this vein for some hours and then the next message from the surveillance team was the one we had been waiting for, it was whispered, "We have visitors." The baddies had arrived!

All my team gathered together in the end room and we went through our plans again, with everyone getting into their allotted place. We received further whispered messages keeping us up to date. The last message told us that one person was on an outside balcony on the first floor of our side of the house. We then heard a window break, a bathroom window just two rooms away from our bedroom. This was going exactly to plan.

The intruder got into the bathroom without any problem. He should then have come out into the corridor just down from us, turned right and away from our position, making his way to the stairs. Once he had gone down the stairs we could deploy along the landing corridor and make sure that he couldn't return to the bathroom and escape. Our bedroom door was set back slightly from the corridor, so we had it open so that in the pitch blackness we would be able to see a torchlight as the offender came out of the bathroom. Then the unexpected happened. Instead of seeing the torchlight going away

139

from us and towards the stairs, it came towards us and we heard him go into the bedroom next to the bathroom. This was next to the bedroom where half the team had been relaxing and two doors away from where we were. At that point one of my officers tapped me on the shoulder and whispered in my ear, "I have left my sandwich box on the bed in the next room." WHAT? How could he? If the intruder went into that room, as it now seemed likely, he would have seen the sandwich box and that could blow it all. There was nothing we could do at this point, we would just have to play it by ear and see what happened.

We amended our plans slightly and then worked on the theory that he would check the room next to ours and, providing the sandwich box didn't spook him, he would be likely to appear in our doorway. His torchlight appeared in the corridor and sure enough it came towards us and he went into the bedroom next to us, fingers crossed about the sandwich box. It was obvious that he was searching the drawers in the rooms looking for valuables. If he looked closely enough, he could have the sandwich box on the bed, although there wouldn't be any sandwiches left, the way Tony ate there wouldn't even be any crumbs! The torchlight appeared again in the corridor and came in our direction. Just as he was about to turn the small corner into our doorway, I called, "STRIKE!"

One of my officers and I jumped out on him and pointed guns at him as all the lights came on. He was told in no uncertain terms to stand still and do as he was told. Despite the absolute horror of the situation he found himself in, apart from the first few seconds when I thought he might have had a heart attack, he took it quite well. He was clearly a professional, said nothing and did exactly as he was told. He was searched but wasn't carrying a gun.

By now with all the noise and lights, our other team from downstairs appeared and were of course delighted at the good outcome. They praised us however, through gritted teeth because we had got the result and not them. They were convinced we had enticed him towards us so that we could have the arrest. As if we would!

In October 1987, I was called out to a firearms incident near Amersham. It was one of the rare times that I was first to arrive at the rendezvous point on a callout, as Amersham police station was so close to home.

A local officer had been sent to a domestic dispute at a farm complex where a young man, an employee working at the farm, was causing trouble. He lived in a caravan in a barn at the farm and had just been told that he would be losing his job and therefore his home as well. Late in the evening he tried to gain access to the farmhouse but the young woman living there with her small child had locked the doors, so he couldn't get in. She reported to the police that he was drunk and shouting and he then started shooting wildly with a shotgun. The local officer entered the farm area and saw the young man who did appear to be drunk. He fired the shotgun in the general direction of the officer. As the officer made a rapid withdrawal from the farm he heard further shotgun blasts. He reported in but remained in the vicinity because of concern for the safety of the young mother and her child. Contact was made with her and she and the child were out of harm's way, locked inside the house.

Once my team and our weapons had arrived we formulated a plan, kitted up and moved up to the farm. On arrival we made contact with the local officers and put an armed containment on the farm. Whilst there had been several more shotgun blasts, it had been quiet for some time and there was no sign of the offender. A first, cursory look at the farmyard showed a car parked near the house which had been subjected to several shotgun blasts, at least six. An attempt at a search of a farmyard complex in the dark, looking for a man who knew the location very well and who was described as drunk and clearly armed with a shotgun and lots of cartridges, presented its own unique problems. Our primary concern was for the safety of the young mother and her child. We implemented that part of the plan and removed them to a place of safety.

There had still been no sounds or sign of the offender and by then we had tight control of the whole area. It could be that he had left the farm before our arrival, but the local officers had done a good job in an outer containment and we believed that he was still somewhere within the farm complex. It was not long before dawn, so we waited for the first signs of light and then commenced our search across the farmyard. We knew where his caravan was, tucked into a barn, but it was quite difficult to move towards it safely. However, as we approached we could see a double-barrelled shotgun lying on its side on a hay bale by the caravan door. We suspected that he was probably inside the caravan and hopefully then not a threat with a shotgun. That proved to be correct. Access to the caravan was not easy owing to the lack of space. However, entry was gained without any problems and he was arrested. The situation was helped by the fact that he was lying on the bed in a drunken stupor. He was removed without further incident.

Examination of the shotgun revealed a live cartridge still in the gun. A search of the farmyard culminated in thirteen shotgun cartridges being recovered. The overriding factor was that the situation had been resolved with no-one injured, no shots fired by police and the operation safely completed. Couldn't say the same for the car in the farmyard though, that was a write off.

We were regularly engaged on two somewhat unusual armed operations. These were security operations where we were required to escort a moving load and, because of the nature of the consignment being escorted, it was essential that we were armed.

One of these had no regular pattern and occurred perhaps once or twice a year. We would meet at an Atomic Weapons Establishment (AWE) and be briefed regarding the load we were to escort. It was a nuclear material, Plutonium, which during the process of being used, multiplied itself and at the end of the process there was more than at the beginning. Before this extra material could be used it had to be cleaned, clearly a complicated process. There were three locations in the world where this cleaning could take place, Russia, China and the USA. No surprise then that the UK's material went to America. Owing to the nature of the material and the inherent risk of it falling into the wrong hands, a high security escort was required.

Our convoy consisted of a pilot car going ahead of the main convoy, anything up to a mile ahead, looking for anything unusual or any vehicles of concern, especially at the exit and entrance slip roads at the motorway junctions. The main convoy would be one or two of our vehicles immediately in front of the load-carrying heavy goods vehicles (HGVs) and another one or two immediately behind. We would also have one more of our cars way back behind the convoy, again as much as a mile back, to check for any vehicles which appeared to be monitoring or following the convoy. Most of the police vehicles would be our unmarked cars but we also had two marked traffic cars as part of our convoy. For this operation we would be heavily armed and have extra firepower with us by way of our specialist firearms officers and equipment. We also had the use of our police helicopter which gave the perfect overview of the whole operation.

Our destination was an RAF base outside the TVP area. As we were going to another police force area carrying firearms, we were met at the county border by officers from that police force who would assist by attaching themselves to our convoy. On arrival at the RAF base we were waved straight through to a special area and remained there whilst the load was transferred to an aircraft. Once it had taken off and had cleared UK air space we were free to leave and return to our area. It was imperative to remain until the plane was well on its way, in case there was a problem and it was required to return to base.

After the cleansing of the material in the USA we were notified that the load was being returned to the UK, so we then completed the operation in reverse by escorting the load from the RAF base for its return to the AWE with the same level of high security.

The other armed operation was a little more regular. Approximately once a month, a convoy of vehicles would depart the Bank of England in London with a quantity of old worn banknotes to be taken to a special incinerator elsewhere in the UK, where they were destroyed. Again, the security was high owing to the vast amount of money being carried; it was multi millions of pounds. The convoy was escorted from its base by armed offices of the MPS who took the convoy all the way through to its destination. We joined the convoy and escorted it from our boundary with the Met Police and took it through the TVP area, handing it over to officers from another police force when we reached our border.

The Bank of England vehicles were interesting. There were always at least three HGVs but normally only one or perhaps two of them were load bearing. The other vehicle(s) were dummy vehicles carrying nothing. The reason for this was that if there was an attack on the convoy with the intention of stealing the money, the baddies would not know which vehicle was carrying the high value load. We were never aware which vehicle was carrying the money, they all looked and were staffed the same. In addition, there were several fail safe devices built in to protect the money. The vehicles had an observation window at the front above the driver's cab giving the Bank of England officials on board a clear wide view over the driver's head. They had several controls within their bulletproof observation post in the vehicle. If there had been an attack on the vehicle, by pressing a button within their cab, all the tyres would be blown out and punctured so that it could not be driven away. Another button, if pressed, would set off a dye flooding the area containing the money so that the notes would be dyed and rendered useless. Once these had been activated, a number of alarms and flashing lights would be set off as well as automated messages being sent to various locations saying that the convoy was being attacked.

The heavy weight of the vehicles made the convoy very slow. It needed to be well organised when it was required to change lanes to overtake. It was all controlled by the lead police vehicle and the car to car radio when we all moved out together. Due to the length of the convoy it was inevitable that we would sometimes have a member of the public in their car in our convoy when we were overtaking. It was interesting to see their puzzled looks and bewilderment as we attracted their attention and gave them instructions, normally visually, as to what to do.

Due to the slow movement of the convoy we were with it for quite some time, so we amused ourselves when it was quiet, planning how we could attack the convoy and get away with the money; purely hypothetically of course and for good operational reasons. After all, if we could work out a way of doing it then it was possible that the baddies could as well. Although we had some good ideas, we never (almost never!) came up with one which was a fool proof definitive plan that would have worked. During the many times we were involved with this escort there was never any serious concerns about a potential attack on the convoy. We were suspicious sometimes about certain vehicles and occupants, but we always took pre-emptive action, such as boxing them in and pulling them over for a check. We always had one or if necessary two vehicles allocated to that task if it was needed.

Owing to the nature of the work we were involved in and because of our expertise in certain areas, we often had to change duties at short or nil notice. It became a regular occurrence to receive a message whilst we were working on one commitment to then have that duty superseded by something else taking precedence.

A classic example of this was when I was inspector on Support Group working a night duty tour with two of my parties at Greenham Common, Newbury. We were assisting with a big police operation overseeing the movement of cruise missiles in and out of the air base. It was a regular operation for the missiles to be brought out of their storage at Greenham Common air base and taken in a protected convoy to a different location. The procedures for the deployment of the missiles were then tested in an exercise. There was always a huge protest by the women camped outside the base when this happened, and it was supplemented by hundreds of other protesters against the cruise missiles.

We were waiting for the missile convoy to approach Newbury when I received a message to contact the control room at the police headquarters as a matter of urgency. I pointed out that our operation to get the missiles back into the base was approaching its crucial stage, but they repeated that it was urgent for me to contact them. When I did I spoke to one of the ACCs: it was almost unheard of for him to be at work at that time of night. He told me to take one of the parties of Support Group officers with me and go immediately to (a named) police station. On arrival I was to report to the Superintendent, the officer in charge of the police area, who had been called out from his home and was awaiting my arrival. No, he could not tell me what it was about, all would be revealed when we arrived. Yes, he was aware how important our role was with the cruise missiles, but this was to take precedence, no more discussion, go now.

Taking one of the parties with me we hot-footed it to our new destination. There was a lot of activity within the station; clearly there was 'something' going on. I eventually found the Superintendent whom I knew well; obviously he had been called out from his bed because he had put his uniform trousers on over his pyjamas which were sticking out from the bottom of his trouser legs! Well it was about 2.00am after all. He seemed pleased to see me and said, "I am glad you are here. I can go home now, it's over to you."

I was still confused, "Hold on," I said. "We know nothing. I was told that you would tell me what was going on." He pointed out a man that I had never seen before standing in his office. He introduced him as a nameless person, apparently a high ranking official from somewhere who would tell me everything. He informed me that the Chief Constable was fully aware of the situation and I was to do what this gentleman told me. Well that was different. With that the Superintendent was gone.

I then received a briefing from the man about an event which had been reported in the national news during the day of which I was aware. He gave me detailed instructions of what our immediate task was. He handed me a sealed envelope and told me the location of where we were to go. On arrival I was to be met by a named person who would be waiting for me. I was to hand the sealed envelope to him and tell him not to open it until he had started his journey; he was already aware of his ultimate destination. Once he was under way he could open the envelope which contained detailed instructions for him. He would then leave and we were to wait for approximately thirty to forty minutes before returning to the police station. The unnamed man required assurance that I knew exactly what to do and I confirmed that for him. Apparently, there was nothing more to be said other than would we please get on with it. The still unnamed man then left and there I was with this sealed envelope and nothing more.

Of course, it would have been very tempting to go to one of the many empty offices somewhere in the station, open the envelope to see what it contained and then perhaps replace the envelope with a new one. But that would probably have been the wrong thing to do, perhaps, and it would definitely have been wrong to take a photocopy just so that I had something to keep in case anything untoward happened.

It probably only contained................ well unfortunately further speculation is not possible!

I briefed the Support Group officers; they were as incredulous as I was but they eventually believed me. We completed our task successfully as instructed and to the letter. Our involvement in this most unusual and bizarre incident was over. However, I regret that I am unable to enlighten the reader any further because of the nature of the commitment. I apologise for that. Did it even really happen?

CHAPTER 18

–

Drugs Operations

Where duty calls

We were involved in many drugs operations normally with a specific role. The brilliant job done by Drug Squad officers was quite unique. In the world in which they operated they had to look the part and they most certainly did. The role of Support Group was to do the difficult entry part of any operation; effect access into a drugs stronghold, secure the premises and all the people therein. Then the Drug Squad officers would be called in to bring their expertise to the party. Owing to the nature of such operations and the joint trust required between us, it meant that we got to know the Drug Squad personnel very well and worked closely with them during the planning stages of sometimes quite difficult and complex operations.

Often the drug dealers were armed to protect their stash of drugs and we dealt with that aspect of the operation first, normally executing an armed raid to ensure that the drugs were not disposed of before we gained entry into the premises. It was pointless securing the premises, making contact with those inside and then calling them out if the place was full of drugs. Guess what they would do? They disposed of the drugs by flushing them down the toilet and then the evidence was gone. Yes, that was inconvenient and financially damaging for the drug dealer, but not as bad as being caught by the police and charged with dealing and having the drugs seized and losing them anyway.

A drug dealer, whose stash of drugs may have been worth several thousand pounds, would have taken extreme steps to protect it. That sometimes included being armed with guns and other weapons and protection by armed 'heavies'. We have dealt more than once with a robbery where one drug dealer had attacked another and stolen his drugs. As the 'victim' of the robbery, what could they do? They could hardly report it to the police that as a drug dealer they had been ripped off by one of their own. It was obvious therefore that they had to be self-sufficient with their security and that could present extra problems for us. When we did an armed raid on a drugs stronghold, as we crashed the door in, those inside did not immediately know who it was, the police or other druggies who had come to steal their stash. However, the fact that they may have been armed was just another element we had to take into consideration when we planned such a raid.

In October 1986, after some good observations by the Drug Squad we assisted them in a high-profile raid. It was a public house on the Oxford Police Area. More correctly, it was the car park of the pub. There had been drug dealing on an industrial scale taking place every evening and night in that car park. The potential difficulty was that the nearby housing estate had a reputation for being a possible volatile area and it needed to be dealt with sensitively. The problem we faced was how to 'sensitively' bring fifty police officers, some in riot gear, to the car park of the local pub, normally heaving with people, some of whom did not get on particularly well with the police. There had been quite a number of complaints over several months to the police from some local people, who were fed up with what was going on and wanted it stopped. From the local police commander's point of view such complaints could not be ignored and something had to be done. That was where the expertise of the Drug Squad and Support Group officers were brought to the fore. The secret for the success of this operation was the speed of its execution.

On the evening of the raid, we briefed well away from the pub so that those within the drugs fraternity would not see a lot of police activity and become spooked. Very quietly and quickly, everyone was put in place for the raid and we all knew exactly what our specific roles were. One important job was to ensure that none of the dealers could be allowed to run into the pub, if we had to follow them that could have caused a major problem. If there was to be a confrontation we would have it on our terms outside and not in the pub.

Once everyone was in place, the main dealers were identified and located, and the strike was called. We all appeared as if from nowhere, ran to our appointed positions and it worked exactly as planned. A police presence at the doors to the pub prevented anyone going in and the dealers were captured, still holding their goodies. No injuries, no escapees, no major confrontations, no problems. It was the speed of it all which we had alluded to in the preparation of the plan, which proved vital. It was all over in minutes, eighteen people arrested, their cars secured, and a quantity of drugs seized. It generated a lot of interest with local people coming out to see what was happening. What was especially heartwarming was that many of them congratulated us for taking such decisive action. A good job well done by everyone and some plus points for the local police. The only ones who didn't see it quite like that were the drug dealers of course.

A few months later we were involved in a similarly high-profile operation with potential for major problems if we got it wrong. It was April 1987 and the target for the raids was Mandela Court, Reading. This was a particularly difficult area of apartment blocks, which was a closed off area once inside the Court. In the past, local officers had sometimes suffered when chasing offenders into the Court in an effort to make arrests. Some residents would gather at short notice and give the police a hard time. They were very aware when there was any police activity in the area, therefore a tight working plan was needed to overcome this problem. The Drug Squad had been successful in keeping surveillance and working on gathering intelligence for about nine months. We were involved at the planning stage and it became apparent that it was possible to mount a successful operation to combat the high level of drug dealing taking place in a number of flats well inside the Court.

On the day of the raid, in an effort to firm up the intelligence that showed drugs were available, our first task was to take off a number of punters, that is, members of the public who had gone there to buy drugs. We started in the afternoon, working off information from the surveillance teams; we were given details of vehicles leaving the Court in which it was suspected that their occupants had bought drugs. In our unmarked police cars, we followed the target vehicle until it was clear of Mandela Court and at a suitable distance away, so as not to show out near the Court, we stopped the vehicle. The driver was told that we suspected that he/she had bought drugs and we thoroughly searched the occupants and their vehicle. The information from the surveillance teams was so good that we had a hit every time; drugs, mainly cannabis and/or amphetamines.

All those arrested were taken to Reading police station and interviewed. From those interviews we were able to add to the picture we had already built of what and where things were happening in the Court. It was essential that none of those arrested were released before the raid took place, otherwise they could have blown the whistle to the drug dealers inside the Court. The next part of the plan was to make some test buys. We needed undercover police officers to go into the Court and attempt to buy drugs. Drug Squad officers could not be used as they may have been known by some of the drug dealers, so we tended to use young police officers who had just come out of their initial training. That way they didn't yet look, talk or act like police officers. As they were inexperienced in such matters, we needed to make sure that we were close to back them up if anything went wrong. Fortunately, that part of the plan worked very well. They were able to buy drugs at the door of two flats so that confirmed which of the flats we were going to raid.

The optimum time for the raid was somewhere around 9.30pm and the two flats were going to be hit at the same time. They were in different blocks, but to reach the doors of the flats would take about the same time from each of our hiding places. I was sergeant on Party Four, which was based in the north of the force area and a close friend of mine Paul, known to everyone as PF, was the sergeant on Party Two, based in the south of the force. There had always been a great friendly rivalry between the two of us and the officers of both parties. Wouldn't you know it, I was leading my team into the first flat and PF was leading his team into the other one. We spoke before we set off, with me informing PF that he and his team would have to try and keep up with us because we needed to hit the doors simultaneously. There was similar banter between the teams which was always good sport before we got serious. We then got into position to wait for the 'Go' from the surveillance officers.

At 9.45pm we received the message, 'Go, Go, Go' and we were away. We came out of hiding, ignored everyone in the vicinity and ran to our designated door. One of my officers was the nominated 'door knocker' which he did with great effect, one crash and the door was in. We were aware of the layout of the flat and each officer went to their designated place, shouting as we went. Everyone inside was taken hold of and put on the floor face down, all the time being told what to do and what was happening. This was done to minimise the effect of anyone inside who was in possession of any weapons or if anyone wanted to fight. We were acting under the auspices of a Warrant, which gave us the authority for what we were doing. We were wearing protective equipment including NATO helmets, like a crash helmet with a visor, and carrying long batons. I must admit that looking at and checking the team before we received the 'Go', they looked formidable and more than a little frightening. No wonder then that almost without exception, everyone we came into contact with that evening did exactly as they were told.

Once we had secured the flat and occupants, we brought in different teams to deal with those arrested, any stolen property found and the drugs, of which a large quantity had already been found by us prior to the detailed search of the flat. On checking one bedroom we found it almost impossible to open the door because it was full, and I do mean full, floor to ceiling, wall to wall with brand new electrical goods and other items which had been stolen and used by punters to buy drugs. It took several hours just to log everything in that room.

We could now relax a little and we helped the teams in our flat and escorted prisoners out to the prison vans, once they had been documented. Looking outside, I could see that the whole of Mandela Court was under the control of the police. A total of one hundred and fifty police officers were used in the operation and it had all worked superbly. During this down time, I met with my colleague PF, to discuss how their part of the plan had worked. I was aware that as our door was going in I heard their door go at the same time. They appeared to have had a similar result at their flat and without doubt the whole operation had been a great success.

By this time the documentation of the prisoners, the stolen goods and the drugs was well under way. We had set up a system for this documentation which resembled a supermarket check-out and was almost as busy. In the middle of all that, we received a message that the Chief Constable, Colin Smith, was coming to have a look inside the flats we had raided. That was most unusual, and the teams were overjoyed that he would take the trouble to come and see the success we achieved. A few minutes later the Chief appeared in our flat with the local Superintendent, had a look round, listened to what had taken place and then left without saying anything and I do mean anything, not one word uttered to any of the officers. What a let down, just a word of acknowledgement would have been the icing on the cake. After all that planning, the difficulties overcome, the hard work by everyone involved and the obvious success achieved, he didn't even have the common decency to speak to any of the officers in the flat, just a word would have meant so much. After he left some of the officers were a little deflated. He left them with the impression that either he wasn't bothered, or worse still, he didn't approve of some of our tactics. This was a huge missed opportunity by the Chief. Bad move, Chief Constable, thanks for nothing, you need not have bothered to attend, and I would have preferred it if you hadn't done so.

It is in circumstances such as this which can define and influence the way that you personally conduct yourself going forward as a leader. Watching and learning and storing away the good things but being aware of and dismissing the bad things. A classic case here then of what not to do and how officers should be treated after performing magnificently in a very difficult operation.

At the end of the day thirty-three people had been arrested, with no injuries on either side. A vast quantity of various drugs were seized, as well as a mountain of stolen goods contributing to a completely successful operation.

The following year we were again contacted by the Drug Squad to say that there was a major drugs raid on the horizon. From the first information the indication was that it would prove extremely difficult to get in close to the dealers before the drugs could be disposed of. In the intervening time after the Oxford and Reading major drugs raids, we had worked with the Squad on numerous drugs jobs and developed an expertise in effecting difficult entries to premises. Since the Reading job I had been promoted, left the Support Group for a short time and then returned as inspector Support Group for the south of the force.

I met a Drug Squad intelligence officer who took me to one of the Observation Posts (OPs) which they were using to keep surveillance on some drug dealing. We were in High Wycombe and the dealing was taking place inside and immediately outside, a pub in the town centre. We watched the proceedings for a couple of hours during an evening. It was extremely busy, resembling Sainsbury's supermarket on a Saturday. I am not suggesting that Sainsbury's were involved in drug dealing; it was just the comparable volume of people going back and forth.

Some of the punters did not even bother to go into the pub; the deal took place, quite openly, in the doorway. I could see the problem for us would be getting close to the dealers before they raised the alarm. The pub was situated in the middle of a terrace of flat fronted buildings with no alleyways, just flat buildings with a door leading directly from the street into the pub. There were several different premises and houses either side of the pub, all closed at that time of night, therefore there was no way of having cover for us to get close to the pub doorway. The entrance into the pub was very small and covered at all times by guards for the dealers. Directly opposite the pub was a large public car park, open and flat, with just a narrow roadway between it and the pub, again no cover at all. During the daytime the car park was busy but, after 6.00pm, it was empty. The only cars using the car park were punters, who would park just long enough to go to the pub to score their drugs and leave. During my observations there were always a minimum of six spotters for the dealers. Their job was to be watching all the time and moving about in front of the pub and occupying the doorway. Anyone who went into the pub had to push past them and was almost checked by them before entering. They were some big guys as well. In addition, if anyone parked in that car park for reasons other than going to the pub, a couple of spotters would immediately go up to the car and look in and check it out. They were clearly very surveillance conscious.

The dilemma was plainly obvious, how could we get a large contingent of police officers close enough without being seen and then make it to the doorway and into the pub whilst taking out at least six spotters? It was time to go away and work out some options. We eventually came up with a plan. The two previous major raids in Oxford and Reading were reliant on speed at the crucial moment when we called the Strike for the operation to be a success. This was different. The speed element would come if and when, we could somehow move the spotters away from the doorway so that they couldn't raise the alarm. This was how it worked.

We hired a small number of furniture removal type vans and they would be filled with officers who would be brought in as back up when Support Group had deployed and secured the premises, all the spotters, the guards and everyone inside. The nearest point we could put the Support Group officers was on foot round the first corner from the doorway of the pub. They would be dropped off at that point at the last minute, immediately before the Strike was called. Once they rounded the corner they would have to run the estimated fifty yards to reach the doorway of the pub. The problem being that, as soon as they rounded the corner they were in full view of everyone, not least those spotters. To give them a fighting chance of reaching the doorway without being seen or at least have a head start, we needed a diversion and we had a belter.

One of the Support Group officers had previous experience on the Traffic Department and he was a damn good motorcyclist. I had previously arranged with a well known motor cycle company to visit their headquarters where they would let us have on test one of their latest, biggest, flashiest and most sought after motor bikes. It was also one of their most expensive, so hopefully nothing untoward would happen to it. On the day of the raid I took Tim, the ex-traffic biker, to collect the bike. The company was excellent and handed over the keys to Tim, who thought all his Christmases had come at once. He had clearly fallen in love with it at first sight. It was hard to tell him that it had to go back the next day. As we left with Tim on the bike I told him to try it out and get used to it, maybe I could have chosen my words better. He scorched up the road and disappeared in seconds. I did wonder for a moment if that might be the last I ever saw of him.

Fortunately, he turned up at the briefing, still with the silly grin that I suspect he had been wearing since we collected this impressive machine. He had already been briefed as to what was required from him and we discussed how he could achieve it, but the finite detail of how he did it was up to him. He was a very experienced officer. I was in the OP; it was my job to call the Strike once everything and everyone were in place. By 9.15pm we were all ready to go. There had been a lot of activity at the pub, so it was all looking good. The Support Group was in place, hidden around the corner and ready to go once Tim had done his stuff. I gave him the okay and away he went.

As I looked at the front of the pub, to the right and about one hundred yards away was a petrol station. I heard and saw Tim on the motor bike screeching off its forecourt as he zoomed towards the front of the pub. He stopped before he reached it, performed a wheelie and whilst revving loudly, he shouted abuse at the spotters inviting them to come and have a go if they thought they were hard enough. He picked out one spotter and I think he questioned his parentage. The spotters and everyone else in the vicinity were transfixed by Tim's exuberance; he then turned the bike in the road and roared off. Meanwhile, I had called the 'Strike' and Support Group officers were at the doorway and amongst the spotters, who never saw them coming, not one of them. All the dealers, spotters and guards were detained outside and inside the pub. The backup was called in and police flooded the immediate area. The raid was over in seconds. There was no resistance, no injuries and a quantity of drugs, mainly cannabis and amphetamines were seized. The 'no injuries' needs clarification, there was one injury of note. Pete, one of the raid team, turned his ankle when jumping out of the van but didn't notice the pain at first. His role was to go straight through the pub and with colleagues to clear through to and secure the rear of the pub. That was done successfully without any problems. Once all was secure and presumably with the adrenalin subsiding he was aware that his foot was hurting a lot. His crewmate took him to hospital where x rays showed he had broken a metatarsal in his right foot. It was commendable that he did his job first and then we could attend to his hurty foot.

A total of twenty-eight arrests were made, including a number for dealing in drugs. We had secured overwhelming evidence to prove the offences. The local Community Relations Officer was asked to attend the scene whilst we were still there, and he was very supportive of the action taken and the subsequent result. It had been a very successful operation. Certainly, it had taken quite some time to put it all together, but it proved to be very worthwhile. Well done, Tim, for your vital input at the sharp end causing the diversion. Now if only I could find him and get that motor bike back!

CHAPTER 19

—

Training

One of the best

Due to the specialised nature of the work Support Group officers were engaged in, a great deal of time was devoted to the various types of training. As firearms officers we were required to attend the firearms range for live shooting once every four weeks as a minimum and had to re-classify every time. At the end of the day's shooting, every one of us was retested to the same standard as when we were first authorised to carry a gun. That involved fifty rounds of ammunition fired from various distances at different targets. The qualification being forty-six out of fifty. Anyone who failed to obtain the requisite number of hits was required to attend remedial training within a few days and at that time it was imperative to re-classify. We were very fortunate to have our own indoor firearms ranges at Maidenhead and later Reading. When the huge new police station was opened at Milton Keynes we had a brand-new range there too. We also had the use of an outdoor range in Oxfordshire, where we would train with more specialised weapons such as shotguns and rifles.

In addition to the monthly live firing, we were also subjected to tactical training once a month, this was sometimes delayed owing to operational commitments, especially during our busy periods. This training involved all sorts of exercises working with the police dogs and handlers and other specialists. Occasionally, it would be an open country exercise where we were tasked with finding and apprehending an armed criminal who was somewhere out in the open. For this we worked with the dogs, German shepherds in this case, and their handlers; the dog would track and locate the criminal and then we would take over and resolve the situation. Another time it may have been a criminal or criminals holed up somewhere in a large building. We had the use of disused hospital premises which were perfect but made it very difficult to resolve situations, exactly what was needed in training.

We normally took it in turns to play the bad guys and it was always interesting being on the 'other side' waiting to be found by our colleagues. It was a bit more disconcerting when hiding in a building and waiting to be found by the dog. The situation was that the dog handler briefed the 'criminal' to make sure they were in a cupboard or room with a substantial door and to make sure the dog could not get in, yeah right, as if! Coming to the end of the exercise, the police would be closing in and the dog handler could be heard calling out, "You in the building come out with your hands up or I will send the dog in."

The job as the 'criminal' was to give no indication of where they were located, and the dog was supposed to find them. Soon after that the dog would be released and would search the rooms on its own. For the safety of the dog handler, in case the armed criminal was in the building, he/she would remain outside and wait for the dog to indicate that it had found someone by barking. The next thing the 'criminal' would hear was the dog coming into the room where they were concealed and then sniffing at the door of their hiding place. The dog would then try to get in and at them as it was trained to do. That's when the dog barked to indicate to its handler that it had found someone. Then praying that the door held and hanging onto it for dear life became a good idea, because just the other side of the door was a damn great Alsatian trying to get in. It was always a relief when the handler called the dog back and the armed team came in and made the arrest.

It was brilliant working with the dogs and it filled us with confidence to see how good they were. It was always my ambition to get through the day without being bitten by a dog, something not always achieved. The dog handlers would encourage us to 'run for the dog'. Sometimes it would be used as an initiation for new officers on Support Group; to put the sleeve on, be chased by the beast and brought to the ground. When running for the dog it was important to be properly protected. That entailed wearing at least a heavily padded sleeve on the right arm. The runner would set off, simulating an escaping criminal, the dog handler shouted, "Stop!" (in training the runner never stopped) If the runner continued the dog was then set free to chase him/her down. As the animal closed in, the runner put their arm in the air behind them and the clever dog seized it with those bloody great big teeth and brought them to the ground. A few seconds later, hopefully pretty damn quickly, the handler arrived and called the dog off. It was important to remember to put the arm wearing the sleeve into the air, not the other one!

Early in my Support Group career, I ran for a dog called Sultan. He was a long haired German Shepherd and looked like a bear, he was supposed to be a friend of mine. When I ran for Sultan the first time, I wasn't told how much he enjoyed his work, especially with 'new people' like me running for him. I donned all the protection, set off, heard the dog handler call to me to stop and I then heard Sultan pounding up behind me, eating up the ground. I put my arm back at the right time, but his party trick was to launch himself from behind me and hit me in the back with his front paws, knocking me to the ground. Fortunately, having been well briefed by the dog handlers beforehand of what to do if I fell over, I was able to get my arm up and Sultan, bless him, seized it with those massive jaws. It was great to see at close hand how good, effective and frightening he was. Nice doggy.

I had lots of dealings with Sultan. His handler, Dick, was a friend of mine, we had worked together at Chesham and he lived near me. One Sunday I needed to speak with him, so arranged to call round and see him at his home. My youngest son Matthew came with me and we stayed for a couple of hours. During that time Matthew and Dick's son played with Sultan, who was off duty of course, until they got bored and went outside to play. After I had made a fuss of this huge long haired, bear like dog with lots of stroking, he lay across my feet and went to sleep. I had to wake him to move him when it was time for us to leave. I made arrangements to see Dick and Sultan the next day when he was to be involved in our tactical firearms training day at the old Pinewood Hospital site in darkest Berkshire.

The next day the training was going very well, with several scenarios of finding armed criminals in various locations within the hospital complex. The final one, was to find someone who had fired shots at police and had run into the hospital. We cleared the ground level and then had to tackle the first floor. We reached the top of the stairs and found that the long corridor went left and right with numerous doors leading into rooms, all of which had to be checked. It was perfect for a dog to check those rooms. I was lying at the top of the stairs, with my gun covering the corridor to the right in case the offender suddenly appeared. My crewmate was doing exactly the same covering the left hand corridor. Dick and Sultan were then called to the top of the stairs where Dick would call to the offender and then let the dog go to search all the rooms. Just as Dick, with Sultan on a tight lead, reached me lying flat out on the stairs, Sultan couldn't resist the temptation and bit me on the inside of my thigh, not hard, just a nip and he never broke stride doing it. Dick said it was hilarious, I regret I didn't see it quite like that. He said that as he was bringing Sultan to the top of the stairs, he could see what the dog was going to do but couldn't stop him. He said it was just too tempting, Sultan looked at the two juicy bums staring up at him lying on the stairs and just had to nip one of them and he chose me, his so-called friend, bless him.

Some years later, when the Dog Section was one of the departments I was in charge of, I was visiting their training day and they invited me to run for the dogs again. I tried to explain that I had already done so several times previously years before. The dog handlers knew that but that didn't stop them pressing me. It always looked good if the boss ran for the dogs during training, so that left me with little choice. Dog handlers did like to have a laugh and they had me over that day, big style.

They introduced me to a new dog that had just finished its training, a nice German shepherd, not too big. I tried to make friends with him, in the hope he would remember that I was nice when I ran for him. I was kitted up in the Michelin Man type suit and donned the padded arm. I was ready to go when they put the friendly dog away in its van and brought out a different one, one I had never met before. This was a beast of a dog, looked like a bear and dripped saliva from its huge teeth. And I was supposed to run for THAT? Well I couldn't back out, so I just got on with it and set off running. I heard the handler shout, "Stop or I will release the dog."

My first thought was, 'I will stop and then I will be alright,' but I just kept on running. Then all I heard was the dog panting as it closed down on me, it latched onto my arm and down I went. Those few seconds before the dog handler arrived to get the dog off, as always seemed like an eternity, but I was fine, and it was all over. If anyone ever has the chance to take part in running for a police dog - don't! It is terrifying but only really fun when it's all over.

Training was always the place to find out if new equipment and ideas were going to work. They may perhaps need some 'tinkering with' to make sure everything ran as smoothly as possible when they were implemented as tactics in live operations. It was correct to say that things didn't always go to plan, but the training day was the time to find that out. On one such day, I ended up as the injured person.

We were doing room clearances, as described previously. I was one of the firearms team and we had cornered the last 'offender' in the final room to be checked. He had made it known to us that he was armed and he would not surrender under any circumstances, nor would he be taken alive. The room he was in had no outside windows and no adjoining doors, he had chosen well for his last stand. He was, in real life, one of our firearms instructors so we wouldn't have expected anything less. We formulated a plan and part of that was to keep him engaged in conversation so that we had an idea of his whereabouts in the room. We had armed officers standing either side of the door and the plan was that the door would be crashed open. He would have expected to be confronted by officers standing either side and/or behind the cover of a ballistic shield in the open doorway and he would engage them, that is, open fire on them. What he would not necessarily be expecting was an armed officer lying prone in the doorway. That would have given a vital advantage to the officer on the floor, to see immediately what the situation was as the door went in and if the 'offender' was ready to engage, said officer would have the upper hand and open fire if necessary. The officer lying flat out in the doorway was me.

We were ready. When he last spoke, the 'offender' sounded as if he was at the back of the room and to the left as we looked. On a silent count of three, the door was crashed open and I immediately saw the 'offender' directly in front of me, also lying on the floor. He had rolled out from the right hand side to the middle of the doorway and I found myself staring down the business end of a double barrelled, sawn-off shotgun. I fired two shots and seemingly at the same time he also fired both barrels. I remember seeing the flame and shit coming straight at me. Then I felt the pain. We were all using blanks, but they did kick out flame and other bits from the blank cartridges. Whenever we used blanks we were obliged to wear plastic glasses. Thankfully on this day we were. Bob, the firearms instructor playing the part of the baddie, was using his experience thinking that we would not expect him to be on the floor and he was right. Unfortunately for me, he didn't think that we would employ the same, sneaky tactic.

Replaying it in my mind and discussing it for the debriefing, seeing the twin barrels of the sawn-off shotgun pointing directing at me was alarming; as they stared back at me they seemed huge, like a double entrance to a tunnel. Then the BOOM as both barrels exploded right in front of my face was an experience not to be repeated, once was quite enough! Oh well, no damage done. Well not much anyway, apart from a ringing in the ears from the noise of the guns being fired so close and me picking bits of wadding from the blank cartridges out of my face for the next couple of weeks. Lessons well learnt.

We took the opportunity on training days to become proficient in the use of stun grenades and other specialised equipment and to practise our car drills. That involved armed arrests of people in vehicles and deployment from all sorts of vehicles in armed situations. It was an opportunity to practise and develop new skills which were often required. A strategy was developed for armed entry to buildings on ground, first and second floor rooms. Abseiling was also on the agenda. We would set aside time to work through previously completed operations where things had not necessarily gone exactly to plan, ensuring that we covered every eventuality in order that we would be better prepared the next time. We also worked with the helicopter, being transported quickly to isolated or out of the way locations and using its versatility to spot for us in open country. It was a very physically demanding job at times so to ensure a good level of fitness we had our own assault course which we used to great effect regularly.

The Public Order Training Department was closely linked to Support Group; in fact, a number of the instructors had previous experience as Support Group officers. We supported them during major public order training or riot training, as some people liked to call it and they supported us regularly on operations. Once all the training sessions had finished for the rest of the force, we were subjected to the them, using all the public disorder scenarios. We were really put through our paces by the instructors. It seemed as if they expected more from us because the physicality appeared to go up a notch or two. It was vital to keep up to speed with the latest tactics relating to public disorder; using equipment such as riot shields and long batons and working alongside the horses of the mounted section etc. We had an important function to work closely with officers deployed in riot gear, the PSUs, in the event of dealing with real incidents of public disorder.

We could be used as snatch squads, going into crowds and bringing out the targeted offenders or main organisers or any one of a multitude of tasks. It was essential to know how other officers would be working and what they could and couldn't achieve when petrol bombs were being thrown. It was part of the training to form a three-man unit, each with a riot shield and take cover behind them whilst they were petrol bombed. It did give real confidence once experienced, to know how much protection those shields gave.

I have previously made reference to the camaraderie on Support Group, which was second to none in my experience. There was also friendly rivalry and banter between the officers on the two Northern and two Southern parties. I was in a very fortunate position because I had a foot in both camps, having been a constable and sergeant on the north and an inspector on the south. Whenever an opportunity came to play tricks or 'wind ups' on each other, the challenge was always taken up.

I have mentioned before a friend and colleague, PF, the sergeant in charge of Party Two. He was instrumental in a number of such 'wind ups' but made sure everyone was aware that he could not be caught out by any, he was the man who could not be had. He was suffering a problem with his garden of which most of us were only too well aware. He was immensely proud of his lovely lush green lawn. Apparently it would rival the centre court at Wimbledon on a good day. However he had been troubled with moles burrowing in the lawn and making a real mess of the grass. According to PF he had got the better of the moles, he was too smart for them and all was sorted, mole problem gone.

He had gone on and on and on about the moles, it being the main topic of conversation for several days. As it seemed to have been resolved, two of his team, crewmates Steve and Dinger, thought how unfortunate it would be if the moles were to reappear, given all the time and effort put into the glorious lawn! Much later that evening, knowing that PF's wife and family were away for the night and the house would be empty, they gained access to the garden. It was a clear dry night and pausing only briefly to admire the very well tended lawn, they found the fine earth previously removed from the lawn after the moles had been at work. Guess what they did with that earth before they left?

By the early hours of the morning the shift had finished and PF was given a lift home by a friend and colleague Dave, an ex Support Group officer, now a dog handler. Despite it being around 5.00am Dave was invited in for a cup of tea. By now the rest of PF's team were aware of what had taken place, as was Dave. He later recounted the tale that as PF was at the sink filling the kettle, dawn was just breaking and he was looking out of the kitchen window. There was a bit of a double take, he bent down for a better look, squinting in the half light to get a view of his lawn. He went absolutely ballistic. It was a conspiracy by the mole world aimed specifically at him. The kettle was thrown furiously into the sink, expletives rang around the kitchen as he rushed to unlock the back door and take a closer look at the little piles of earth scattered all over the lawn.

Before going to bed he left a note for his wife who was due home later that morning, to contact the so called expert Mole Catcher, put a flea in his ear and get him back to sort it out. The Mole Catcher duly arrived later that day and finding that the 'mole hills' had no mole holes, declared to PF the immortal words, "I think you've been had"! and indeed he had, at last.

The story of course spread like wildfire throughout the Support Group and even wider in TVP. A week or so later on arriving at TVP HQ for a briefing, one of the ACC's, some of whom were not known for their sense of humour, pulled alongside PF's car and asked him with a smile, "How are your moles"? Classic.

EPILOGUE

—

In October 1991, having served for four years as an inspector on Support Group and a total of fifteen years in the three different ranks, my time was up and I had to move on. It was a sad day for me, ending my time on the specialist department which I had worked so hard for and enjoyed so much. However, it was quite right and proper, because of the highly specialised nature and the intensity of the work, there were restrictions on how long one could serve with the Support Group.

Since joining this department in 1975 for the first time, I had seen some dramatic changes in policing in general, but also in the specific type of policing I had been associated with. There had been some tremendous successes in the numerous, diverse and difficult operations, events and enquiries I had been involved in. I met and worked with some of the very best and most talented police officers who ever served in the Police Service. There had of course, been sad and tragic and frustrating times, but they were far outweighed by the enjoyment and satisfaction of doing a successful job and achieving excellent results. Working closely with colleagues, in difficult and often dangerous situations, formed a lasting bond. It had been a privilege to serve alongside them and I am proud to have done so, some of whom would remain friends forever. Eventually everyone has to move on, and sadly, my time was now.

I was very fortunate to be posted to High Wycombe as inspector in charge of operations. It would be quite a change for me to once again work mainly regular hours and I would also have an office to operate from rather than working out of my briefcase from the boot of a police vehicle.

I was looking forward to this change of direction and new challenges.
It would be a different type and style of policing but my involvement in interesting, complex and difficult work was not yet finished, as I was soon to find out...

GLOSSARY

—

ACC	Assistant Chief Constable
ARV	Armed Response Vehicle
CHOGM	Commonwealth Heads of Government Meeting
CBRN	Chemical Biological Radiological and Nuclear
CID	Criminal Investigation Department
FA	Football Association
HGV	Heavy Goods Vehicle
HMP	Her Majesty's Prison
HO	Home Office
IRA	Irish Republican Army
MP	Member of Parliament
MPS	Metropolitan Police Service
MUFTI SQUAD	Minimum Use of Force Tactical Intervention Squad
OP	Observation Point
PC	Police Constable
PM	Prime Minister
PSU	Police Support Unit
PSV	Public Service Vehicle
RCS	Regional Crime Squad
RUC	Royal Ulster Constabulary
SAS	Special Air Service
SEG	Special Escort Group
SOCO	Scenes Of Crime Officer
TVP	Thames Valley Police
WPC	Woman Police Constable

PEN PICTURE

—

Mervyn Edwards was born in Banbury, Oxfordshire in 1947. He fulfilled a boyhood dream in 1971 when he became a Police Officer and joined Thames Valley Police.

With little more than three years service he joined Support Group, a specialist department with the primary function of dealing with firearms incidents. He would remain with the department for fifteen of the next eighteen years serving in three different ranks including time as a Firearms Tactical Advisor.

In 1995 Mervyn was promoted to the rank of Superintendent and took command of the policing for the Newbury Bypass. At that time, this was a unique and highly challenging policing operation. The sheer scale and scope of the civil protest had never previously witnessed such organised disapproval, objections and demonstrations. His innovative and imaginative approach saw him propelled on to the national protest guidelines working group. He was highly commended for his work during this time.

He was later part of a small cadre of specialist Firearms and Public Order Commanders. He was also part of the National Police Working Group tasked with preparing the Police service in the UK to deal with Chemical, Biological, Radiological and Nuclear Terrorism (CBRN). His experience, knowledge and professionalism within these specialist areas required him to make regular appearances as a keynote speaker in the UK and USA.

He retired in March 2002.

He lives in Buckinghamshire and is married to Geraldine with two grown up sons Gareth and Matthew.

5th May 2018